Health, Wellness, and Physical Fitness

BY
DON BLATTNER AND LISA BLATTNER

COPYRIGHT © 1997 Mark Twain Media, Inc.

ISBN 1–58037–022–5

Printing No. CD-1819

Mark Twain Media, Inc., Publishers
Distributed by Carson-Dellosa Publishing Company, Inc.

Table of Contents

Introduction

Health and physical education today are quite different than just a few years ago. They are no longer just courses devoted to physical activity and hygiene. Today, many look on health education as a lifelong process that can enable students to live happier, more productive lives. This process includes regular exercise, proper nutrition, abstaining from substance abuse and smoking, and developing a balanced mental outlook. All of these factors comprise a person's lifestyle.

People who choose a healthy lifestyle live longer, have a positive sense of well-being, and generally have happier lives. Choosing a healthy lifestyle early in life has many benefits. Proper nutrition and exercise dramatically diminish the chances for disease, disability, and early death. The lifestyles adopted early in life are likely to carry over to later life, so the earlier one adopts a healthy lifestyle, the greater the benefits.

The purpose of this book is to teach students to make informed decisions for a lifetime of fitness and wellness. Students will be asked to study and evaluate their current lifestyles and then be shown how their lifestyles could affect their future health and happiness. They will learn that their future health depends on many factors, such as hereditary risks, exercise, and proper nutrition. They will learn that their future health is also affected by being able to avoid certain things, such as tobacco, illegal drugs, excessive use of alcohol, and communicable diseases. They will also learn that they must maintain positive mental outlooks, become wise health consumers, and learn to avoid accidents as well as deal with emergencies.

A second purpose of this book is to give students an opportunity to begin keeping records of their health and fitness information. Keeping vital information concerning one's health is a lifelong task, and the sooner one begins, the better. For this reason, it is recommended that students be encouraged to keep health notebooks or folders. The exercises are designed not only to provide an understanding and appreciation of health and fitness, but also to be used for lifestyle decisions in the future. A health notebook will give students a reason to record valuable health information for themselves and make it easy to apply their knowledge for improving the health of their families.

**Several forms throughout the book are provided so students can collect data about their health and their family medical histories. THESE ARE NOT TO BE USED AS ASSIGNMENTS. Medical information is personal, confidential information, and students should keep these forms at home in their health notebooks or folders.

Lifestyle and Longevity

There is no way to accurately predict exactly how long a person will live. We do know, however, that one's lifestyle and habits play an important part in **longevity**. Longevity means the length or duration of a person's life. People who smoke have a shorter average life span than those who don't smoke. Lean people usually live longer than those who are overweight. People who exercise regularly live longer, healthier, more active lives than those who don't. Remember, we are talking about averages and are not referring to a specific person. For example, you may know someone who is 85 years old, has smoked for 65 years, and is in apparent good health. While such cases do exist, they are rare. Much more common are smokers who die of heart attacks, lung cancer, or emphysema before they are 65 years old.

Insurance companies have access to a great deal of information concerning people—how they live and how they died. They are able to use this information to make general statements concerning the consequences of certain habits and lifestyles. Northwestern Mutual Life, an insurance company, has taken this information and developed a quiz to give people an idea of how their lifestyles could affect how long they might live. The quiz is called *The Longevity Game*. This quiz should not be interpreted as a scientific instrument that will accurately predict the length of a person's life. Rather, it should be used as a guide to indicate how certain habits or lifestyles have the potential to shorten one's life. It is hoped that by understanding these factors that could potentially shorten your life, you will be encouraged to make changes that will enable you to live a longer and better life.

THE LONGEVITY GAME

The Longevity Game was developed by Northwestern Mutual Life and is used with their permission. Your family and friends may also play *The Longevity Game* by going to Northwestern's website at (http://www.northwesternmutual.com/games/longevity/longevity-main.html). *The Longevity Game* is an interesting quiz that asks individuals to examine their lifestyles and other factors in an attempt to predict how long they will live. Of course, no one can predict the exact length of a person's life, and this quiz is not meant to be taken literally. However, information available from health organizations, medical studies, and insurance companies indicates that certain factors have a significant effect on one's length of life. The purpose of *The Longevity Game* is to illustrate how a change in lifestyle can increase your odds of living longer.

Directions: Complete *The Longevity Game Quiz.* Since the quiz is appropriate for people of all ages, for fun you might imagine you are 20 years older than you are. How do you look? What is your lifestyle? See how these changes might change your longevity. Also, you may want to give *The Longevity Game* to your parents so you can compare your longevity potential to your parents' scores. Why are the scores different? What changes might you or your parents make in order to improve the scores?

Everyone starts with an average life expectancy of 73 years and adds or subtracts the appropriate number of years from their score as they respond to *The Longevity Game* questions. Keep your quiz in your health notebook or folder for future reference.

1

HEALTH NOTEBOOK   Name _____   Date _____

The Longevity Game

Beginning Age _____73_____

AGE

Women generally live longer than men. Recent figures show that newborn girls will live seven years longer than newborn boys. At age 60, on the average, women live 3 years longer than men. Also, how long you have already lived is a good predictor of how long you may live.

Scoring

	Men	Women
Age 25 and under	Add 0	Add 7
Ages 26-40	Add 1	Add 7
Age 41-50	Add 2	Add 7
Age 51-55	Add 3	Add 7
Age 56-60	Add 4	Add 7

Age 60-88: Men add 4, plus one year for each two full years over age 60.
Women add 7, plus one year for each two full years over age 60.
Ages 89 and Over: Men, your age plus 3 years. Women, your age plus 5 years.

Now, add or subtract the appropriate number of years from your beginning age.

Updated Age _____

FAMILY HISTORY

Family history influences longevity. Like gender and age, it is a factor over which you have no control. However, knowing the medical history of your family may help you identify potential problems and minimize related risks.

- If both parents survived to 70 with no cardiovascular (heart and blood vessel) problems before age 60, add 2 to your score.
- Cardiovascular problems or death of a parent before age 60, subtract 1.
- Two or more brothers or sisters with cardiovascular problems, subtract 1.
- Parent, brother, or sister with diabetes since childhood, subtract 1.
- Family history unknown, add 0.

Updated Age _____

EXERCISE

An active lifestyle is good insurance against heart disease, a common cause of death.

- If you have a job requiring physical activity, or if you make both physical activity and some sport a regular part of your day, add 3 years.
- If you lead an "average American" lifestyle with little physical activity, add 0.
- If you are sedentary—that is, if you take escalators instead of stairs, ride a lawn mower, or drive your car to get to stores a few blocks away, subtract 3 years.

Updated Age _____

HEALTH NOTEBOOK   Name _____ Date _____

STRESS

Stress can be a cruel master or a helpful servant. Knowing how to handle stress makes life more enjoyable.

- If you use stress as a positive influence in your life, add 1.
- If you have your share of ups and downs, add 0.
- If you often feel stress using you, subtract 1.

Updated Age _____

BLOOD PRESSURE

High blood pressure cannot be cured, but it can be controlled. Following a sound medical regimen can produce good results, while tobacco and fatty foods may aggravate blood pressure.

- If you know your blood pressure, add 0—if you don't, subtract 2.
- If you have your blood pressure checked regularly and it is normal, i.e., it is less than 140/90, add 3.
- If you have high blood pressure and are on medication, your physician indicates that it is under control, and you take your medication or follow other restrictions imposed by your physician, subtract 1.
- If you have high blood pressure and don't take your medication regularly, your physician says your blood pressure is not under control, or you require frequent changes in medication, subtract 6.
- If you have high blood pressure and you smoke or have elevated cholesterol, subtract an additional 3.

Updated Age _____

DRIVING

If an accident occurs, a fastened safety belt offers reliable protection. Responsible drivers drive defensively. Auto accidents rank fourth overall as the most common cause of death in the United States and are the leading cause of death through age 34. About half of all auto accidents are alcohol-related. Driving drunk is not only suicidal, it's murderous.

- Drivers who have had no moving violations or accidents in the past three years, add 1.
- Drivers who have had four or more moving violations or accidents, which were not alcohol-related, in the past two years, subtract 4 years if age 16–34, and 2 years if age 35 or older.
- Drivers who have been convicted of driving under the influence of alcohol in the past five years, subtract 6.
- Drivers who have been convicted of driving under the influence more than once in the past five years, subtract an additional 6.
- Drivers who always wear safety belts, add 1.

Updated Age _____

HEALTH NOTEBOOK   Name _____   Date _____

SMOKING

Almost 350,000 deaths per year are related to the effects of smoking. The risk of lung cancer and heart disease declines immediately when one quits smoking. If you:
- Never smoked, add 2.
- Quit more than 2 years ago, add 1.
- Quit less than 2 years ago, subtract 1.
- Smoke 2 or more packs per day, subtract 8.
- Smoke less than 2 packs per day, subtract 4.

Updated Age _____

DRINKING

Heavy drinking can affect one's health adversely, and it contributes to auto and job-related accidents. How often you drink is as important as how much you drink. If you:
- Never drink more than three drinks in a day, add 1. (One drink equals twelve ounces of beer, a five-ounce glass of wine, or $1\frac{1}{2}$ ounces of 80 proof spirits.)
- Drink five or more drinks one or more times a week, subtract 6.
- Drink three or four drinks three or more times a week, subtract 3.

Updated Age _____

DRUGS

Taking drugs is an ill-advised way to have a good time and one of the best ways to lose *The Longevity Game*.
- If you use hard drugs like cocaine or narcotics, it's time to evaluate your lifestyle, not your longevity.
- If you never use drugs for "recreation," add 1 year.

Updated Age _____

DIET

Cholesterol contributes to heart disease, and saturated fats help produce cholesterol. Vegetables, fruits, cereal grains, and starches contain no cholesterol and little or no saturated fats.

Your age matters here.

If you are:
- A light user of saturated fats: eat red or organ (brain, kidney, liver) meats and eggs, one to two times per week, add 2 if under 60, add 1 if over 60
- An average user of saturated fats: eat red or organ meats at least four times per week, add 0 if under 60, add 0 if over 60
- An indiscriminate user of saturated fats: eat red or organ meat and eggs seven or more times per week, subtract 2 if under 60, subtract 1 if over 60

Updated Age _____

HEALTH NOTEBOOK   Name _____ Date _____

WEIGHT

Avoid being overweight by eating right and exercising regularly. Refer to the weight chart below to determine how close you are to your suggested weight.

If you are:
- Within 10%   Add 2
- 11%–19%   Add 0
- 20%–39%   Subtract 2
- 40%–59%   Subtract 4
- 60%–79%   Subtract 8
- 80%–100%   Subtract 14

THE LONGEVITY GAME WEIGHT CHART

Weight measured with shoes and street clothes.

MEN

Height	Ideal Weight*	10%	20%	40%	100%
5.0	140	154	168	196	280
5.1	142	156	170	199	284
5.2	144	158	173	202	288
5.3	146	161	175	204	292
5.4	148	163	178	207	296
5.5	150	165	180	210	300
5.6	152	169	182	213	304
5.7	155	171	186	217	310
5.8	158	174	190	221	316
5.9	161	177	193	225	322
5.10	164	180	197	230	328
5.11	167	184	200	234	334
6.0	170	187	204	238	340
6.1	173	190	208	242	346
6.2	176	194	211	246	352
6.3	179	197	215	251	358
6.4	182	200	218	255	364
6.5	185	203	222	259	376
6.6	188	206	226	263	376

*Weight which correlates with best longevity.

WOMEN

(% OVERWEIGHT)

Height	Ideal Weight*	10%	20%	40%	100%
4.9	117	129	140	164	234
4.10	119	131	143	167	238
4.11	121	133	145	169	242
5.0	123	135	148	172	246
5.1	125	138	150	175	250
5.2	127	140	152	178	254
5.3	130	143	156	182	260
5.4	133	149	160	186	266
5.5	136	150	163	190	272
5.6	139	153	167	195	278
5.7	142	156	170	199	284
5.8	145	159	174	203	290
5.9	148	163	178	207	296
5.10	151	166	181	211	302
5.11	154	169	185	216	308
6.0	157	173	188	220	314

Final Age _____

This is your estimated longevity according to the lifestyle factors you have indicated in the game. Think about what changes you could make to increase your longevity.

Name _____ Date _____

HOW DO I SPEND MY TIME?

We have seen in *The Longevity Game* that your lifestyle greatly affects your life and well-being. A healthy, happy, well-adjusted person usually has a balanced lifestyle that includes adequate rest, exercise, work, and social activities. How do you spend your day?

Shown below are two circle graphs. The circles represent one day, or twenty-four hours. Divide Circle A with the percentage of time you spend on each of the following activities each day:

1. Sleep or rest   _____
2. Work   _____
3. School   _____
4. Homework   _____
5. Exercise   _____
6. Family   _____
7. Friends   _____
8. Alone   _____
9. Other   _____

For example, if you spend six hours sleeping each day, then mark one-fourth of the circle and label it "Sleeping," since six is one-fourth of twenty-four.

Circle A

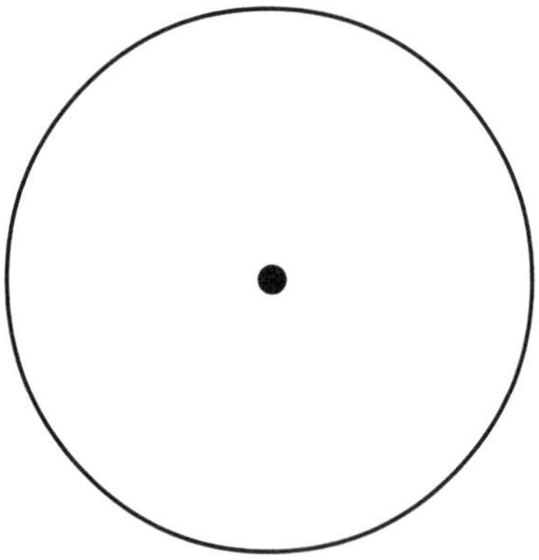

As you look at Circle A, do you think you spend your time wisely? What criticisms do you have of the way you spend your day?

_____
_____
_____
_____
_____
_____

Circle B

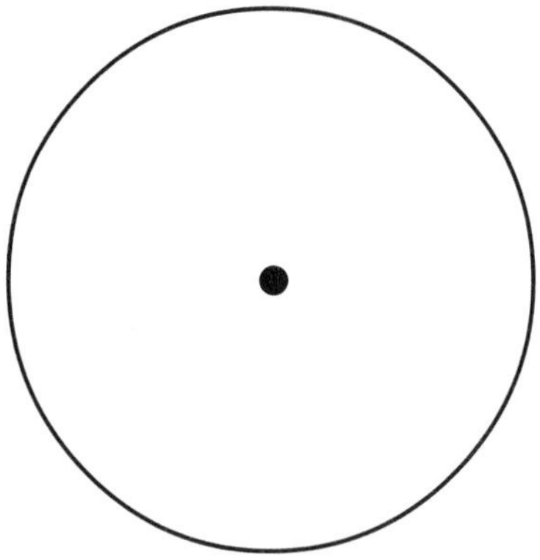

Divide Circle B to create what you feel would be the ideal way to spend your day. What changes did you make in Circle B? Why?

_____
_____
_____
_____
_____
_____

Heredity

Families have a history which includes the health, behavior, and appearance of our ancestors. Like the history of a country, a family's history provides useful information in understanding the members of the present family. For example, suppose your parents and several of your aunts and uncles had heart attacks when they were relatively young. This knowledge is very important. It does not mean, of course, that you will necessarily have heart problems, but this knowledge may encourage you to consult a doctor for tests to see if you have any symptoms of heart disease and to ask him what steps you can take in order to avoid heart problems.

MENDEL'S EXPERIMENTS WITH PEAS

In order to understand heredity and how it works, it is important to discuss the work of Gregor Mendel, a nineteenth century Austrian monk. He was a mathematician, a scientist, and a teacher. Mendel gained his place in history and in science by pursuing his hobby, which was gardening. Over the years, Mendel observed that plants produced offspring with the same characteristics. For example, if he planted seeds from tall plants, tall plants grew. If he planted seeds from short plants, short plants grew. Other characteristics such as smooth or wrinkled seeds or the color of flowers were also passed from one generation to another.

Mendel also observed that when plants with different characteristics were planted near each other, the offspring from their seeds were not as predictable. For example, if he planted tall plants next to short plants, harvested those seeds, and planted them, not all of the resulting plants would be tall. A few would be short. He wondered why. Was it coincidence? Was the offspring mixture of tall plants and short plants random? Or was there a natural law that would enable a scientist to predict how often a short plant would be produced from the seeds of a tall plant that had grown next to a short plant?

Mendel decided to study and compare sweet peas that were identical in every way but one characteristic, so he could discover if there was some order to the offspring. Mendel's first task was to produce plants which he called **purebreds.** These were plants that would only produce offspring with the one characteristic Mendel was studying. A *tall* purebred, for example, would only produce seeds that would result in tall plants; a *short* purebred would only produce seeds that would result in short plants; a *white flower* purebred would produce seeds that would only result in plants that had white flowers. He produced purebred plants by growing plants that had the characteristics he was studying and then covering each plant with cloth, so that it could not be accidentally pollinated by another plant.

The next year he planted these seeds, and as he suspected, the new plants had the same characteristics of the original plants. The seeds from the tall plants produced tall offspring; the seeds from the short plants produced short offspring. Mendel then decided to **crossbreed** these new plants. He took pollen from tall plants and pollinated short plants. The resulting seeds of this crossbreeding were called **hybrids.**

When Mendel planted seeds from the short plants that had been pollinated by tall plants, he discovered that all of the resulting plants were tall. Nevertheless, he suspected

MENDEL'S EXPERIMENTS WITH PEAS (CONTINUED)

that, although all of the hybrid plants were tall, they might somehow produce some short plants since they originally came from short plants. In order to check his theory, Mendel carefully covered these second generation plants, so they could not be pollinated by another plant. When they developed seeds, he planted them.

The third generation plants that grew from these hybrid seeds produced a pattern of three tall plants to one short plant. Mendel continued his study for several years and repeated this experiment with other characteristics, such as the color of the flower and the smoothness of the seed, and he always got the same result—the characteristics of offspring from hybrids resulted in a pattern of three to one. Mendel decided the characteristics that resulted in three of the plants were **dominant** factors, since three of the four plants would exhibit these characteristics. He called the characteristic that was exhibited in the one plant the **recessive** factor. In his experiments with plants, for example, the tendency to be tall was a dominant characteristic and the tendency to be short was recessive.

Mendel's discoveries were published in 1866. Here are some of his results:

- Crossbreeding does not produce **blending.** Many people believed if a tall and a short plant were crossbred, the resulting plants would be medium-sized plants.
- Characteristics and traits are passed from both parents.
- Some characteristics are dominant and some are recessive. Although the recessive characteristic is hidden, it is still part of the genetic makeup of the plant and may show up in future generations.
- Inherited characteristics and traits are not random, but result in a predictable pattern of three to one. The chances of a dominant trait being expressed in an offspring is three times greater than a recessive trait being expressed in an offspring.

MENDEL'S RESULTS

1. *Parental generation*   TALL   SHORT

2. *First generation hybrid*   TALL

3. *Second generation hybrid*   TALL   TALL   TALL   SHORT

1. The parental generation is a tall plant and a short plant.
2. Plants produced from these parents are hybrids that are tall, but carry genes for shortness.
3. Hybrid plants produce offspring in a ratio of three to one: three plants exhibit the dominant characteristic and one exhibits the recessive characteristic.

Name _____ Date _____

HEREDITY AND EYE COLOR

- Shown below is a chart for three families. The father in each family has brown eyes, and the mother in each family has blue eyes. The father does not have a recessive gene for blue eyes.
- Brown is the *dominant* trait for the color of eyes, and blue is the *recessive* trait.
- The children in each of the families marry, and they become parents.

1. Fill in the coloring of the eyes of all those in the chart. Use "BR" for brown and "BL" for blue.

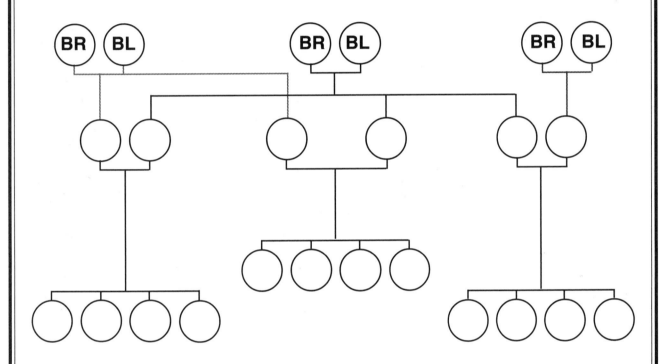

2. In your own words, explain how you determined the eye coloring for each offspring.

_____

_____

_____

_____

_____

_____

HEREDITY AND HEALTH

While Mendel showed that heredity played an important part in physical characteristics of living organisms, it wasn't until much more recently that scientists have discovered genes are also instrumental in determining health and behavior. In the early part of the twentieth century, a Danish botanist named Wilhelm Johannsen named the heredity factors that are linked together on every chromosome **genes.** Each gene occupies a specific place on a chromosome and decides a particular characteristic. The science of studying genes is called **genetics.**

Genetics is one of the most exciting fields of science today. In the 1970s, scientists began genetic experiments with plants. Plants with genes for specific desirable features are being developed. Scientists are developing crops that are resistant to disease or insects, tolerant to drought, or more nutritious. This branch of study is called **genetic engineering** and is important to those who study genes in humans. Scientists are now trying to identify specific genes that carry tendencies toward certain diseases. Once identified, the next step will be to alter these genes so that people who have them will either not contract the diseases or be cured.

This type of science and medicine may seem like science fiction, but scientists are rapidly identifying which genes are related to which characteristics, and doctors and scientists are currently conducting **gene therapy** experiments. In gene therapy, diseased cells are extracted from the organism, altered, and then replaced. At the present time, our limited understanding of genes does not enable us to cure or avoid disease through gene therapy, but we can use our understanding of heredity in order to create a healthier lifestyle.

Almost daily, scientists learn how genetics and diseases are related. Some of the diseases that seem to be influenced by heredity include allergies, alcoholism, Alzheimer's disease, asthma, several kinds of cancer, diabetes, and heart disease. This list is just a sample. New connections between genes and health problems are being discovered constantly. If people are aware that some of these health problems or diseases "run in the family," they can create lifestyles that will minimize their risks. They can also see physicians early and specifically request screenings for the types of problems found in their families.

10

COMPILING A HEALTH NOTEBOOK

In order to keep track of your health and fitness and be better able to deal with illnesses when they occur, you should begin compiling a health notebook or folder in which you can keep such information as health records, food diaries, and emergency numbers. Pages marked with "HEALTH NOTEBOOK" will be given to you to fill out and keep in your notebook or folder. The notebook should be kept at home where you can easily retrieve the information when you need it. Remember, your personal health information is confidential, so no one else needs to see it.

LEARNING YOUR FAMILY HISTORY

Since knowing your family's health history is so important to your own health, what's the best way to discover the health problems your family members have dealt with? The first step is to interview family members in order to discover chronic health problems that relatives have had and that might have eventually killed them. Some of these problems will include alcoholism, cancer, diabetes, heart disease, high blood pressure, obesity, respiratory problems, and stroke.

You will, of course, only be interested in **blood relatives**. Blood relatives are relatives who are genetically related to you. Relatives who are related by marriage are not blood relatives and would not share any of the same genes that you have. For example, your mother's sister is a blood relative, but her husband is not. Your brother is a blood relative, but your stepbrother is not.

Listed below are some guidelines you should consider as you interview relatives concerning their health and their recollections of the health of other family members.

1. Understand that some people may be reluctant to discuss family health problems with you. They may regard illness as a weakness or might feel that certain problems are something to be ashamed about. In fact, you may well be asking them to reveal family secrets that have been hidden or denied for years.

2. Make it clear that your questions are not just idle curiosity, but rather an attempt to learn about health problems that you might inherit.

3. Explain that the information you are collecting is for your use only and will not be shared with anyone else.

4. Listen for hidden messages that might contain clues as to real problems that may concern you. For example, an older family member may say "Uncle Bill was a little absentminded as he got older." You might ask for examples of his absentmindedness or other details to see exactly how bad his memory was. You might also check with other relatives to discover if his forgetfulness was the normal kind that most people experience or if it could be the symptom of a more serious disease, such as Alzheimer's disease.

5. Memories do fade over the years, so as you interview other relatives, try to verify information you have gathered.

6. If a relative is unable to specifically name the disease someone had, list the symptoms, and check them against your family medical history. You may see a pattern of similar symptoms among your relatives.

HEALTH NOTEBOOK

FAMILY HISTORY QUESTIONNAIRE

Here is a form to be kept in your health notebook you may use in order to gather your family medical history. Begin with your immediate family: yourself, your brothers, sisters, and parents. Then go up your family tree as far as possible: aunts, uncles, grandparents, brothers and sisters of grandparents, and so on. You will need a copy of this form for each family member.

After you have gathered all of the information for your family members, you may use the forms to build a medical family tree, shown on page 14.

VITAL STATISTICS

Name _____

Relationship to Me _____

Birth Date _____ Height _____ Weight _____

Marital Status _____ Spouse's Name _____

Number of Children _____ Boys _____ Girls _____

Level of Education _____ Occupation _____

Age at Death _____ Cause of Death _____

MEDICAL STATISTICS

Medical Problems

List all known medical problems such as cancer (type), diabetes, heart disease, stroke, and high blood pressure. Include age at which the problem was first noticed.

Chronic Problems: _____

_____

_____

_____

Accidents: _____

_____

_____

_____

Other: _____

_____

_____

_____

_____

HEALTH NOTEBOOK

FAMILY HISTORY QUESTIONNAIRE (CONTINUED)

Mental Health

Type of Personality: (Nervous, Anxious, Relaxed) _____

_____

Interaction With Others: (Sociable, Quiet, Loner) _____

_____

Behavior: (Happy, Optimistic, Depressed) _____

_____

Other Mental Concerns: _____

_____

_____

Lifestyle and Personal Habits

Did the person:

1. Smoke? What did he/she smoke? How much did he/she smoke? How long did he/she smoke? Did he/she ever quit?

_____

_____

_____

2. Drink alcohol? What did he/she drink? How much did he/she drink? How long did he/she drink? Did he/she ever quit?

_____

_____

3. Have a special diet? What kind of food did he/she generally eat?

_____

_____

4. Exercise? What kind of physical activity, including job and sports, did he/she participate in?

_____

_____

5. Have special hobbies or pastimes?

_____

_____

HEALTH NOTEBOOK   Name _____   Date _____

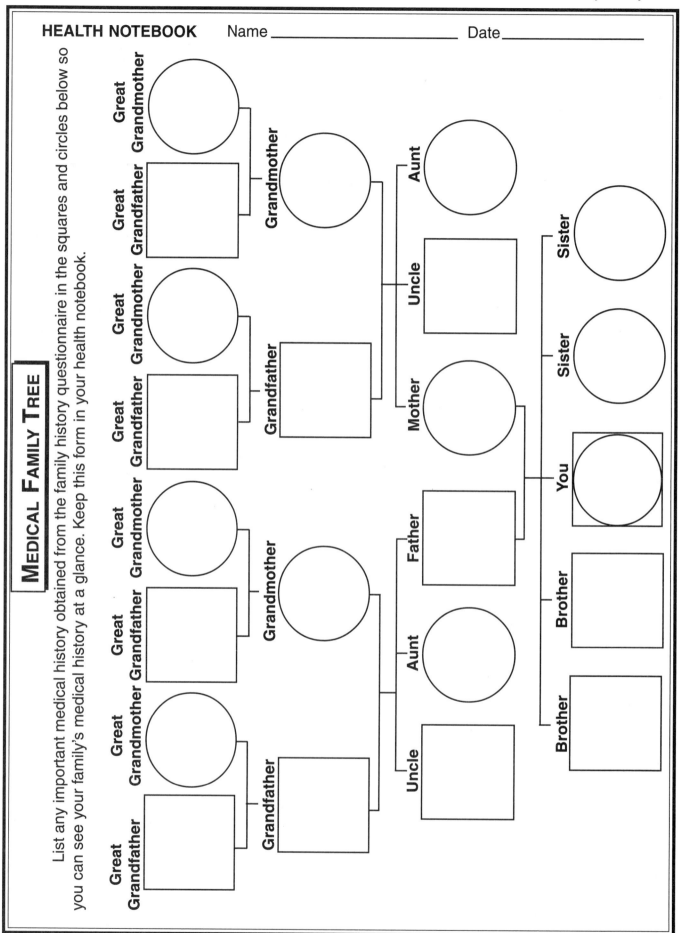

MEDICAL FAMILY TREE

List any important medical history obtained from the family history questionnaire in the squares and circles below so you can see your family's medical history at a glance. Keep this form in your health notebook.

Exercise and Fitness

Almost every day on television, one can see salespeople trying to sell food supplements, pills, or products guaranteed to make you thinner, healthier, stronger, more attractive, and help you live longer. After a few months, when the salesperson has sold as much of the product as he/she can, the item disappears and is replaced with a new product guaranteed to do the same. A skeptical person would say "There is no such wonder product. Nothing can do all of those things the salesperson promises." The good news is the skeptic is wrong. There is something that can make you thinner, healthier, stronger, more attractive, and help you live longer. The better news is this product is free, easy and fun to use, and available to everyone. It's called regular **exercise**. Regular exercise will do all of these wonderful things for you and more.

While doctors and scientists have known for years that exercise is a vital part of a happy and healthy lifestyle, they are still discovering all of the benefits that can be realized from an active life. The Surgeon General lists in a report two great benefits of regular exercise. It enables you to live longer, and it enables you to live better. If exercise only enabled us to live longer lives without improving the quality of the years, the effort may not be worth it. Who would want to be old, feeble, and depressed, with no energy? While we all want to live a long time, we also want to be vigorous, alert, and happy. Exercise allows us to do both.

TYPES OF EXERCISE

There are three ways that exercise helps improve your body. Exercise increases your **strength.** Strength is the capacity of work your muscles are able to perform. Lifting weights is an example of a strength exercise. Other strength-building exercises include boxing, canoeing, football, gymnastics, hockey, horseback riding, judo, rowing, running, sailing, skating, skiing, soccer, squash, swimming, and tennis.

Exercise also increases your endurance or **stamina.** Stamina is the ability to work for extended periods of time. Exercises that can be sustained steadily over long periods of time are called aerobic exercises. Long distance running is an example of an aerobic exercise that builds stamina. Other stamina-building exercises include basketball, boxing, cycling, dancing, football, gardening, gymnastics, brisk walking, hockey, jogging, rowing, running, skating, skiing, soccer, swimming, and tennis.

Finally, exercise improves your flexibility or **suppleness.** Suppleness is the ability to stretch, twist, and bend into different positions. Stretching is an example of a suppleness-building exercise. Other suppleness-building exercises include dancing, gymnastics, judo, climbing, sailing, skating, skiing, soccer, swimming, table-tennis, tennis, and yoga.

EXERCISE AND YOUR BODY

A balanced exercise program, which includes exercises that will improve your strength, stamina, and flexibility, should be a part of your everyday routine. You must realize, however, that age and physical problems may prevent you from doing all types of exercises. It is possible, though, to be physically active and fit at any age.

Promotes psychological well-being. Those who exercise have more energy, breathe better, and experience more restful sleep. They also function better mentally, have better memories and have improved reasoning abilities.

Improves resistance to cold

Reduces the risk of death from heart disease. Regular physical activity decreases the risk of cardiovascular disease and coronary heart disease. If you have a heart attack, your chances of survival are improved if your body is strong from regular exercise.

Helps older adults become mobile and avoid falls. There is some evidence that physical activity makes a person more active and less susceptible to falls.

Improves the length and quality of your life. Longevity may be improved by only moderate exercise. Simple activities such as gardening, dancing, walking, swimming, bowling, and household chores will improve the length and quality of your life if they are done on a regular basis. Also, exercises may be just as beneficial when they are done in several short sessions as when the same total amount of exercise occurs in one longer session.

Reduces feelings of depression and anxiety. Exercise not only relieves the symptoms of depression and anxiety, there is evidence that it may also reduce the risk of developing depression and anxiety.

Prevents or delays the development of high blood pressure. Reduces blood pressure in people with hypertension.

Reduces the risk of developing diabetes. Regular physical activity lowers the risk of developing non-insulin-dependent diabetes mellitus and seems to stabilize the blood sugar.

Improves muscle strength. Age is no barrier to improving strength in one's muscles.

Helps control weight. Increasing physical activity while maintaining the same level of caloric intake results in a reduction of fat cells. Also, exercise builds muscle. A muscular body burns more calories even at rest than one that is not muscular.

Reduces the risk of colon cancer. Regular physical activity is associated with a decreased risk of colon cancer, and evidence is accumulating that it may prevent other types of cancer as well.

Improves flexibility or suppleness.

Helps build and maintain healthy bones, muscles, and joints. It may benefit those with arthritis. Including weight-bearing activities is also essential for normal bone development during childhood and adolescence and for achieving and maintaining peak bone mass, which is essential in preventing osteoporosis.

Name _____ Date _____

EXERCISES FOR DIFFERENT AGE GROUPS

Choose three appropriate exercises for each of the individuals listed below. Assume they each went to the doctor for a physical examination, and the doctor said they were fit enough to begin an exercise program.

1. An 18-year-old man who wishes to make his body more muscular.

_____

_____

2. A 38-year-old woman who wishes to lose 20 pounds.

_____

_____

3. A 55-year old man who has survived a heart attack and wants to improve his cardiovascular system.

_____

_____

4. A 40-year-old woman whose 75-year-old mother has osteoporosis and who is worried she may be similarly afflicted when she becomes 75.

_____

_____

5. An 80-year-old woman who wants to remain as fit as possible.

_____

_____

6. A 47-year-old woman with arthritis who wishes to improve her flexibility, range of motion, and strength.

_____

_____

HEALTH NOTEBOOK   Name _____ Date _____

BEGINNING AN EXERCISE PROGRAM

You are convinced that if you exercise regularly it will improve your health, fitness, and extend your life. What is your next step? What kind of program is best for you? How do you work exercise into your daily schedule? How do you stick with your program? What kind of results do you expect?

FITNESS EVALUATION

Before you begin your exercise program, you need to see how fit you presently are.

Step 1: Estimate your current level of fitness by circling the appropriate number below. "10" means that you are perfectly fit. "1" means that you are not active at all.

Your Present Level of Fitness

Strength	1	2	3	4	5	6	7	8	9	10
Stamina	1	2	3	4	5	6	7	8	9	10
Flexibility	1	2	3	4	5	6	7	8	9	10

Step 2: Using the same scale above, place an "X" on the level of fitness you would like to achieve.

Step 3: Write your overall goal. Do you want to lose weight? How much? Do you want to be able to jog four miles? Do you want to be able to do 50 push-ups?

Goal: _____

_____

Step 4: What do you intend to do to reach this goal? You might want to write the method or program you choose to achieve your goal.

Program to follow in order to reach the goal: _____

_____

_____

_____

_____

_____

HEALTH NOTEBOOK   Name _____ Date _____

FITNESS EVALUATION (CONTINUED)

You may also design a weekly chart similar to the one below that will help you realize your goal.

List Types of Exercise and Time Spent on Each		
Day 1		
Day 2		
Day 3		
Day 4		
Day 5		
Day 6		
Day 7		

Step 5: How long do you expect it will take you to reach this goal?

Time expected to reach the goal: _____

COMMON REASONS FOR NOT STAYING FIT

Problem: Lack of time to exercise.

Remedy: Plan exercise into your daily schedule. Make out a weekly schedule of all your activities. On the calendar, include every activity and the time you plan to spend doing them. After the weekly schedule is completed, note all of the blank spaces. These are places you can write in your exercise times. Write in the specific exercises you intend to include. Spread the sessions out over the entire week. Longer sessions could be reserved for more intense workouts with apparatuses such as weights or activities such as jogging. Shorter sessions could include walking or short aerobic exercises.

Problem: Difficulty in reaching goal.

Remedy: Set realistic goals. Don't try to achieve too much too soon. Exercise should be fun and challenging. It should not be so difficult that you don't want to continue.

Problem: Difficulty in seeing progress.

Remedy: Design your goals so that you are able to actually see the progress you are making. It may take months to reach a goal, but if you are able to see that you are improving your fitness and are approaching the goal, then you will be inspired to continue.

Problem: Losing interest once goal is achieved.

Remedy: Once your goal has been achieved, create a new goal. This will renew your interest in keeping fit.

Problem: Becoming bored.

Remedy: Vary your exercises in order to sustain your interest. You may also find a friend to exercise with you.

Problem: Becoming exhausted.

Remedy: If you are exhausted, you should reduce the kind or amount of your exercise. You should feel energized when you finish exercising, not worn out.

Problem: Losing interest.

Remedy: Give yourself a reward for sticking with your program. Promise yourself that if you stick with the program for a certain length of time, you will buy yourself something.

Name _____ Date _____

Exercise Quiz

Read the sentences listed below. If the sentence is true, circle the letter "T" before the sentence. If the sentence is false, circle the letter "F".

1.   T   F   Senior citizens should not exercise. The danger outweighs any benefits.
2.   T   F   Unless you work up a sweat, there are no benefits to your exercise.
3.   T   F   Exercise helps prevent osteoporosis, a disease in which the bones become porous and are easily fractured.
4.   T   F   You should be in good physical shape before you begin any exercise program.
5.   T   F   You should consult a physician before you begin any exercise program.
6.   T   F   Older people who exercise are more active and less susceptible to falls.
7.   T   F   "No pain, no gain." A good exercise causes discomfort.
8.   T   F   Exercise should be fun!
9.   T   F   Expensive workout clothing and equipment are essential to an exercise program.
10.   T   F   Exercise relieves the symptoms of depression and anxiety.
11.   T   F   Unless you can work out for a long period of time, you shouldn't bother.
12.   T   F   It is not wise to drink water during a physical activity.
13.   T   F   It is best to work out by yourself.
14.   T   F   Regular physical activity increases the risk of cardiovascular disease.
15.   T   F   Lifting weights is an example of an aerobic exercise.
16.   T   F   Exercise should be a part of your everyday routine.
17.   T   F   Your exercise program should include exercises that will improve your strength, stamina, and flexibility.
18.   T   F   There are no risks to vigorous exercise.
19.   T   F   Stamina is the ability to work for extended periods of time.
20.   T   F   Exercises that can be sustained steadily over long periods of time are called aerobic exercises.
21.   T   F   Long distance running is an example of an aerobic exercise that builds stamina.
22.   T   F   Exercise enables a person to live a longer life, but does nothing to improve the quality of the years.
23.   T   F   One should engage in a wide variety of activities in order to keep workouts interesting.
24.   T   F   With an exercise program, it is best to set realistic goals and to chart your progress.
25.   T   F   Vary the location in which you work out.

21

Communicable Diseases

If you were to look around your house, you would probably think that everything was very clean and sanitary. However, if you were to look under a microscope, you would see millions of germs. **Germ** is a general term used to designate a microbe that is harmful to humans. This type of microbe is called a **pathogen**. Microbes are in the air, on everything you have contact with, in the water you drink, on the food you eat, on your body, and even inside your body. While most microbes are not harmful, pathogens can cause disease and make you sick. Fortunately, your skin keeps out most of the pathogens. Unless there is a cut or scratch, it is difficult for germs to enter your body. Some pathogens, though, enter your body when you eat, drink, or when you touch your mouth after coming in contact with someone who is infected. When any of these things happen, you might get sick. If you do develop an illness from a pathogen, it is called a **communicable disease**. There are several kinds of pathogens that cause communicable diseases, but the two kinds most of us are familiar with are **bacteria** and **viruses**.

There are different kinds of bacteria. Some varieties are helpful and are used in the production of cheese, yogurt, sauerkraut, and pickles. However, bacterial action can spoil meat, vegetables, milk, and other dairy products. Some varieties of bacteria cause diseases such as pneumonia, food poisoning, tetanus, strep throat, cholera, lockjaw, leprosy, tuberculosis, typhoid fever, and diphtheria. Medicines to kill bacteria have been developed and are called antibiotics. An **antibiotic** will kill certain types of disease-producing microorganisms or prevent them from growing or reproducing without harming the patient. Nineteenth-century French chemist Louis Pasteur was the first to observe an antibiotic effect. He discovered that certain bacteria can kill anthrax germs. Later, German bacteriologist Rudolf von Emmerich discovered a substance that killed the germs of cholera and diphtheria in a test tube. It was not useful, however, in curing disease. Sir Alexander Fleming, a British bacteriologist, discovered penicillin in 1928. Penicillin is successful in killing many different kinds of disease-bearing microorganisms and is widely used. While antibiotics have been very successful, their wide use has caused the development of many strains of bacteria that are resistant to these antibiotics. Scientists are searching for new antibiotics that will kill these bacteria that have become resistant to the old kinds of antibiotics.

Viruses are smaller than bacteria and can only grow and reproduce in living cells. While many viruses are not harmful, some varieties can make you very sick. Some of the very serious diseases caused by viruses are rabies, polio, and yellow fever. Many viruses, however, cause diseases that are less serious, such as the common cold, influenza, measles, mumps, fever blisters, chicken pox, shingles, and warts. One type of virus is called a retrovirus and causes Acquired Immune Deficiency Syndrome, commonly known as AIDS.

Antibiotics are generally ineffective in treating viruses, so doctors use **vaccines** so people will become **immune** and not develop the disease. One way a person develops **immunity** is by developing a disease and then recovering. Once you get measles or chicken pox, for example, you will never get them again. The reason is the white cells of your blood fight measles and chicken pox viruses by making **antibodies** to kill the germs. Even though you recover from these diseases, the antibodies stay in your body and fight any new

Name _____ Date _____

Communicable Diseases (continued)

measles or chicken pox viruses that get into your body. While contracting a disease and then recovering from it may make a person immune, it is obvious that it would be better if the person did not get the disease in the first place, since some viruses can cause severe disabilities or even death. British doctor Edward Jenner discovered a better way in 1796. He inoculated patients with cowpox and discovered that those who were inoculated became immune to smallpox. Pasteur used Jenner's ideas to develop vaccines used to prevent disease.

When a person is **vaccinated**, a weakened form of a virus is injected into the patient. The virus is so weak that it cannot cause the disease, but it will cause the white blood cells to make antibodies to fight the virus so that the patient becomes immune. Another method of creating immunity is to inject a vaccine made from **dead viruses.** One problem with this second method is that the body's reaction is not as strong as with weakened, but live, viruses. Because the body's reaction is not as strong, **booster shots** are needed from time to time in order to maintain immunity. Some vaccines may also be taken orally.

COMMUNICABLE DISEASES QUIZ

Fill in the blanks with the following diseases.

Acquired Immune Deficiency Syndrome (AIDS), Chicken Pox, Colds, Hepatitis, Influenza, Measles, Mononucleosis, Mumps, Lice, Pneumonia, Ringworm, Scabies, Strep Throat, Sty, Tonsillitis, Tuberculosis

1. _____ is sometimes called "flu." This disease is spread by contact, by coughing and sneezing, or talking. Symptoms include chills, _____ fever, aches, headache, sore throat, cough, and fatigue.

2. _____ are a common illness caused by viruses. They are most common in winter, and a person may have as many as four or _____ five of these a year. Symptoms include a sore throat, sneezing, watery nasal discharge, aches, and fever.

3. _____ is a comparatively mild childhood disease that causes a headache, a slight fever, and a rash, which turns into itchy blisters _____ that contain clear fluid.

4. _____ is caused by the HIV virus . When this virus invades the body, it attacks the immune system, enabling disease to invade the _____ body.

5. _____ is a disease that usually occurs in childhood and is identified by an eruption of red spots on the skin and a fever. It lasts about _____ three days.

Name _____ Date _____

COMMUNICABLE DISEASES QUIZ (CONTINUED)

6. _____ sometimes referred to as "mono," is also called the "kissing disease," because it is spread by the oral-respiratory route. Mono is not very contagious.

7. _____ There are two varieties of this disease: A and B. Both viruses attack the liver, causing an inflammatory reaction. Symptoms include nausea, vomiting, fever, loss of appetite, and jaundice. Jaundice is a yellowing of body surfaces and the whites of the eyes.

8. _____ are small parasitic insects that can live on a human host.

9. _____ is a parasitic skin infection caused by the itch mite. Pregnant female mites tunnel into the skin and deposit their eggs, which hatch after a few days and group around the hair follicles.

10. _____ affects the salivary glands, which are located in the cheek area in front of the ears. When infected, these glands swell, giving the person an unusually puffy appearance.

11. _____ is a skin infection caused by fungi that invade only the dead skin tissue. Infection by one fungus produces raised rings on the skin. However, many other fungi cause different symptoms. Athlete's foot is an example.

12. _____ is an acute infection of the lungs caused by bacteria or viruses. Symptoms include shaking chills, chest pain, cough, fever, and headache.

13. _____ is caused by one form of streptococci bacteria. Symptoms include a sore, red throat, fever, swollen glands (which are not accompanied by a cough), laryngitis, or a stuffy nose. When not treated, rheumatic heart disease may develop.

14. _____ is an inflammation of the tonsils.

15. _____ sometimes called TB, is primarily a lung disease, but it can strike many other organs and tissues in the body. The threat of TB, though diminished from what it was at the turn of the century, may be on the increase in certain parts of the United States.

16. _____ is an infection that forms on the eyelid.

Noncommunicable Diseases
HEART DISEASE

Not all diseases are caused by microbes or pathogens. Some diseases occur over a period of time. These diseases are called **noncommunicable** or **chronic**. Two major noncommunicable diseases are heart disease and cancer. Heart disease kills more Americans than any other disorder. Heart disease is a general term that includes cardiovascular problems such as high blood pressure, congenital defects, infection, narrowing of the coronary arteries, and problems of heart rhythm.

Of all of the forms of heart disease, the principal one is **atherosclerosis**, which occurs when fatty deposits called **plaque** build up on the inner wall of the coronary arteries. This process occurs over many years, and the gradual narrowing of the arteries is often not apparent to the person who is developing the problem. When the disease is advanced, however, a person may experience shortness of breath when climbing stairs or exercising, or they may feel a tightness or pain in their chest called **angina pectoris**.

At some point, the plaque may become thick enough to completely close the coronary artery, cutting off the oxygen to the heart. When this occurs, it is called an **occlusion**. An occlusion can also occur when a piece of plaque breaks away and becomes stuck at some point in the artery. When this happens, it is called **thrombosis**. These two occurrences are the major causes of heart attacks.

Plaque buildup in the artery walls is due to many factors. Heredity plays a big part. Some families are more susceptible to the problem than others. Diet can also be a factor. Consuming large amounts of animal fats and cholesterol increases the odds that plaque will develop. Other factors include lack of exercise, smoking, and stress.

People with angina caused by a narrowing of the arteries can be treated with drugs. Another option is a surgical procedure called **angioplasty**, in which a small balloon is inflated in the blocked artery. The plaque is pressed back against the artery, and blood is able to freely flow again. If the blockage is too great to be treated with drugs or angioplasty, a person may need to undergo surgery known as **coronary bypass surgery**, in which a section of vein is taken from the leg and is sewn into the blocked coronary artery to form a bypass around the blocked area. Patients with severely diseased hearts may need **heart transplants**. These operations are risky, however, because the patient's immune system naturally tries to reject the transplanted heart. Medicines to stop the immune reaction of the body are used, and some heart transplant patients have survived for many years.

Experiments with artificial hearts and heart transplant primates have been tried, but so far these techniques offer no real alternative to the more traditional methods of treating heart disease.

Recently, some doctors have suggested atherosclerosis could be effectively treated by drastically **changing one's lifestyle**. By adopting a low-fat vegetarian diet, strenuous daily exercise, meditation techniques, and other life-changes, plaque buildup can not only be stopped, it can be reversed. The problem is that the change in lifestyle is so drastic, many people have trouble sustaining the regimen for the rest of their lives.

Assignment: Use an $8\frac{1}{2}$ x 11-inch sheet of paper folded in thirds to create a "healthy heart" brochure. Include illustrations, facts, charts, and anything else you think will help inform people about how to maintain a healthy heart.

CANCER

Cancer is not one disease, but a group of related diseases that begin as a single cell that grows and multiplies uncontrollably and eventually forms a lump or mass called a **tumor**. While most cancers develop into tumors, not every tumor is cancer. The tumors that are cancer are called **malignant** tumors. The tumors that are not cancer are called **benign** tumors. What makes malignant tumors so deadly is their ability to spread to healthy cells beyond the site of origin.

Like heart disease, cancer does not have one cause. There are a number of factors that contribute to its development. Heredity, diet, gender, viruses, radiation, chemicals, environmental factors, and immune system deficiency are all involved in the development and progression of cancer.

Cancer is the second leading cause of death in the United States. The types of cancer that cause the largest number of deaths in the United States are lung cancer, colorectal cancer, breast and uterine cancer in women, and prostate cancer in men. The most common cancer is cancer of the skin.

DETECTION AND DIAGNOSIS

Early diagnosis of cancer is important. Here are the seven danger signs of cancer:

• A sore that does not heal
• Change in bowel or bladder habits
• Unusual bleeding or discharge
• Thickening or lump in breast or elsewhere
• Obvious change in a wart or mole
• Indigestion or difficulty in swallowing
• Nagging cough or hoarseness

TREATMENT

The most common methods of treating cancer are **surgery**, **radiation**, and **chemotherapy**. When **surgery** is used, all of the malignant cells, as well as the tissue that might become malignant, are removed during a surgical operation. Many cancers are too advanced to be treated by surgery, or their location may make surgery impractical. When this occurs, another treatment must be used. **Radiation** therapy uses gamma rays and X-rays in order to kill the cancer. Radiation is beneficial when the location of a tumor is where it cannot be removed because surgery would damage essential adjoining tissue. Radiation is sometimes used in combination with surgery. It may shrink the tumor and make surgery easier or possible. **Chemotherapy** is the use of drugs or chemicals to treat cancer. Since the drugs travel throughout the body, chemotherapy is most effective for tumors that have spread beyond the area accessible by surgery or radiotherapy. Chemotherapy is also sometimes used in combination with surgery or radiation.

Name _____ Date _____

FACTORS THAT CAUSE CANCER

Prevention is a person's best approach to avoiding cancer. Listed below are the definitions of some of the primary factors that cause cancer. Use the terms in the word bank below to fill in the blanks to indicate the factor being described.

1. _____ is responsible for 85 percent of lung cancer cases among men and 75 percent among women. People who heavily engage in this activity have lung cancer mortality rates 15–25 times greater than those who do not.

2. _____ are the cause of almost all of the more than one-half million cases of nonmelanoma skin cancer developed each year in the U.S. There is evidence that exposure to this factor is a major cause in the development of melanoma. Those living near the equator are the most at risk.

3. _____ , while legal for adults, is a substance that can cause oral cancer and cancers of the larynx, throat, esophagus, and liver when consumed heavily.

4. _____ is a habit-forming substance used frequently by baseball play-ers. It increases the risk factor for cancers of the mouth, larynx, throat, and esophagus.

5. Excessive exposure to _____ can increase the risk of cancer. This factor is present in medical X-rays. Most X-ray machines, however, are designed to deliver the lowest possible dose.

6. _____ is associated with many cancers. A high-fat diet may be an ingredient in the development of breast, colon, and prostate cancers. Obesity may increase the risk for colon, breast, and uterine cancers. Foods with vitamins A and C may lower the risk for cancers of the larynx, esophagus, stomach, and lung. High-fiber foods may reduce the risk of colon cancer. Salt-cured, smoked, and nitrite-cured foods have been associated with esophageal and stomach cancer.

7. _____ is a female hormone. As a woman ages, she stops producing this hormone and supplemental pills to replace this hormone may be prescribed by a physician. There is some evidence that this hormone supplement may increase the risk of some cancers. A woman and her physician need to decide if replacement of this hormone is best.

8. _____ is a term used to describe the hazards associated with a person's occupation or workplace. Exposure to chemicals, such as mercury, nickel, chromate, asbestos, vinyl chloride, and others, increase the risk of cancer.

WORD BANK

Estrogen	**Smoking**	**Diet**
Chewing Tobacco	**Environmental Hazard**	**Alcohol**
Radiation	**Ultraviolet Rays**	

Name _____ Date _____

NONCOMMUNICABLE DISEASES AND DISORDERS QUIZ

Fill in the blanks with the following diseases: **Anorexia Nervosa, Appendicitis, Asthma, Bronchitis, Cerebral Palsy, Diabetes, Down Syndrome, Epilepsy, Hemophilia, Muscular Dystrophy, Pleurisy, Rheumatoid Arthritis, Scoliosis, Sickle-Cell Anemia, Tendinitis.**

1. _____ is an infection of the bronchial tubes.

2. _____ is a disorder that inhibits voluntary movement.

3. _____ is a lateral curvature of the spine. This disorder occurs most commonly during the adolescent growth period.

4. _____ is usually found among adolescent girls who diet excessively and unsafely, which causes them to become abnormally thin.

5. _____ is an inflammation of the appendix.

6. _____ is actually a group of progressive diseases that produce a breakdown in muscles, causing weakness and making movement difficult.

7. _____ is a respiratory disease. An attack occurs when the muscles surrounding the bronchial tubes go into a spasm, which reduces the size of the airway. Sufferers may gasp for air and feel like they are suffocating.

8. _____ is an inherited disease that almost exclusively affects African Americans.

9. _____ is distinguished by an increase of sugar in the blood and urine. The pancreas fails to secrete enough insulin to utilize sugar. There is no known cure.

10. _____ is a chronic disease characterized by inflammation of the joints.

11. _____ is a birth defect. Those afflicted have an average IQ of 50 and usually have small heads and slanted eyes.

12. _____ is an inflammation of the tendons around various joints.

13. _____, a nerve cell disorder, is characterized by seizures. The three kinds of seizures are called grand mal, petit mal, and psychomotor.

14. _____ is an inherited bleeding disorder. A patient's blood is unable to clot and a simple cut may lead to death.

15. _____ is an inflammation of the membrane that lines the chest cavity and covers the lungs, often occurring as a result of an infection in the lungs.

Tobacco

Tobacco plants are indigenous to the Western Hemisphere and were first smoked and inhaled by the ancient Maya Indians of southern Mexico. The Mayans brought the practice of smoking tobacco to the North American Indians, where Christopher Columbus observed them using it in ceremonies in 1492. Tobacco seeds were taken to Spain and eventually to England, where Sir Walter Raleigh made the smoking of tobacco in pipes a fashionable pastime. Smoking spread throughout Europe and eventually made its way to other parts of the world.

WARN THE ENGLISH OF THE DANGERS OF TOBACCO

Suppose you were around when Sir Walter Raleigh brought tobacco back to England. Also, suppose you knew about all of the dangers associated with smoking that we know today. The citizens of England, of course, would not be aware of the health risks associated with smoking. How would you warn them?

You could write a letter to the editor, create an advertisement in a newspaper, design a poster to be displayed in an inn, or write a speech to be given at a public meeting.

Your assignment is to choose one of these options. After you have chosen the option you think would be most effective, use this method to warn the English. In other words, if you think making a poster would be the most effective method, make a poster. If you think a speech would be most effective, write a speech.

NOTICE: All Fashionable Lords and Ladies

Take Heed This Warning!

New Evidence About the Smoking of Raleigh's Tobacco

- *The nicotine in tobacco can become addictive.*
- *Smoking causes lung and heart diseases.*
- *Smoking causes cancer.*

TOBACCO AND YOUR BODY

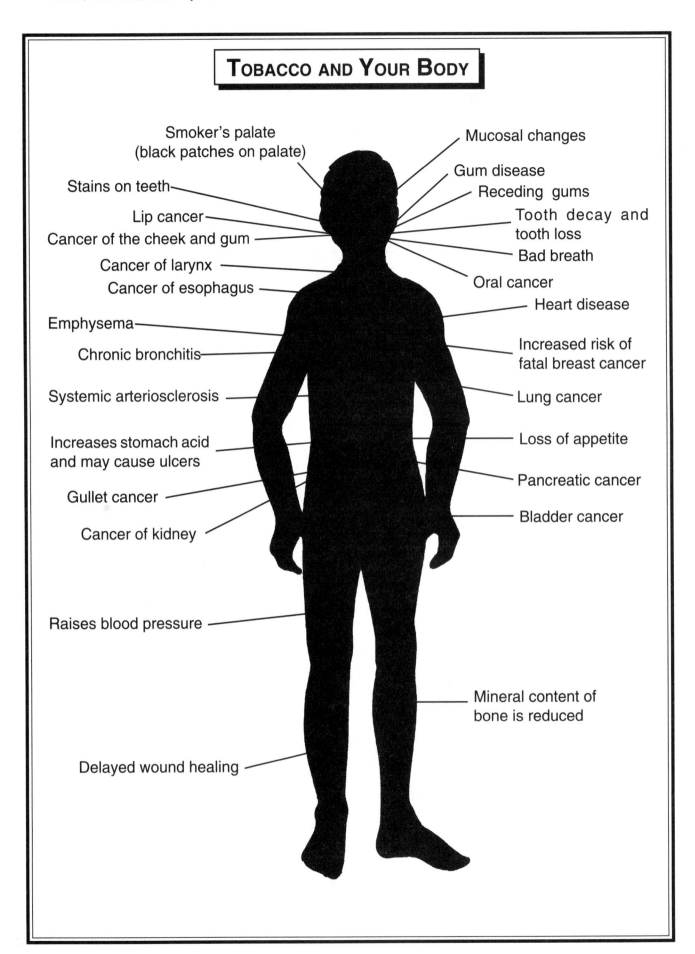

Smoker's palate
(black patches on palate)

Stains on teeth

Lip cancer

Cancer of the cheek and gum

Cancer of larynx

Cancer of esophagus

Emphysema

Chronic bronchitis

Systemic arteriosclerosis

Increases stomach acid
and may cause ulcers

Gullet cancer

Cancer of kidney

Raises blood pressure

Delayed wound healing

Mucosal changes

Gum disease

Receding gums

Tooth decay and
tooth loss

Bad breath

Oral cancer

Heart disease

Increased risk of
fatal breast cancer

Lung cancer

Loss of appetite

Pancreatic cancer

Bladder cancer

Mineral content of
bone is reduced

SMOKING CROSSWORD PUZZLE

Name _____ Date _____

Use the clues below and any other available sources to complete the puzzle.

ACROSS

1. Nicotine causes the blood vessels to constrict, which increases your _____ pressure.
5. Smoking tobacco in a _____ may be related to lip cancer.
6. An open sore in the lining of the stomach that may be caused by smoking.
7. _____ and teenagers of both sexes seem to be smoking more.
10. Smoking may damage this tube, which allows the passage of food from the pharynx to the stomach.
14. Preschoolers whose mothers smoked during pregnancy have significantly lower ____ scores than children of nonsmokers.
16. An inflammation of the mucous membrane of the bronchial tubes, which may be caused by smoking.
17. Smoking causes drastic changes in the ____ system, which is responsible for converting foods into the nutrients the body needs to survive.
18. Smoking can lead to cancer of the larynx and esophagus because it irritates the membranes of the _____.

DOWN

2. Smoking may be harmful to this organ, which is responsible for processing drugs, alcohol, and other toxins and removing them from the body.
3. The softening and thinning of bones that may be caused by smoking.
4. Smoking may be harmful to this system, which protects the body from foreign substances.
8. A liver disease that may be caused by smoking.
9. A burning sensation located in the middle of the chest that may be caused by smoking.
11. Smokers' mouths are very dry because of a decrease in this.
12. Smoking causes the progressive limitation of airflow in and out of these organs.
13. A woman's risk of dying of this type of cancer is increased by 25 percent if the woman is a smoker.
15. A lung disorder, which may be caused by smoking, that results in labored breathing and increased susceptibility to infection.

WRITING A TRUTHFUL CIGARETTE COMMERCIAL

Cigarette ads were banned from television in January, 1971. Until that time, young, attractive people, such as athletes, models, and movie stars, were used to promote smoking in television advertisements. Beautiful women in bikinis smoked at the beach or before a roaring fireplace in a ski lodge with other gorgeous people. Handsome, rugged cowboys smoked as they rode their horses. Tobacco companies delivered the message "Smoking is the sophisticated thing that young, successful, attractive people do. If you want to be like these people, you should smoke. Smoking is the 'in thing' for young people." Obviously, none of these ads showed the real consequences of smoking over many years. What if they had? What would the ads look like?

Create a one-minute television commercial that tells the truth about smoking. It can be serious or it can be humorous. Use the form on the next page for your commercial. The left side of the form is for the video which is the picture or what the audience will see during the commercial. The right side of the form is for the audio. The audio is the sound or narration the audience will hear during the commercial. You may need to make a copy of the form if you have more information to include.

You might want to use some of the facts shown below for your commercial.

- Using this product is one of the largest self-inflicted risks a person can take.
- Tobacco is responsible for more premature deaths and disabilities than any other substance.
- On average, cigarettes shorten your life by six and one-half years.
- The ingredients in this product are the basic cause of 1,000 deaths a day.
- Cigarettes increase your chances of dying between the ages of 26 and 65 by about 100 percent.
- Smokers are 70 percent more likely to die of coronary artery disease.
- Smokers are 1,000 percent more likely to die from lung cancer.
- Smokers are 500 percent more likely to die of chronic bronchitis and emphysema.
- Smokers suffer from more respiratory infections, such as colds.
- Seven times more people die from using tobacco than our annual death toll from highway accidents.
- This product will stain your teeth, and users often have bad breath.
- A pregnant woman who smokes has a higher percentage of stillbirths, more spontaneous abortions, and more premature births, and more of the infants die a few weeks after birth. Their children's physical and intellectual development may also be adversely affected.
- Tobacco is habit-forming, and withdrawal symptoms include tension, irritability, restlessness, depression, anxiety, difficulty in concentrating, overeating, and insomnia.
- Tobacco is so dangerous that warning labels are required by law.

After you write the commercial, you may want to actually make a video recording of it as if it were a real commercial.

Name _____ Date _____

CIGARETTE COMMERCIAL	
VIDEO	**AUDIO**

Alcohol

People consume alcohol in three primary kinds of beverages: **beer**, which is made from grain; **wine**, which is made from fruits; and **spirits**, which are distilled beverages such as whiskey, vodka, and gin. All of these drinks can become addictive, and while a few drinks will not harm most people, excessive alcohol can cause many health problems, including premature death.

How alcohol affects a person depends on many factors. A small amount of alcohol consumed over a long period of time will have little noticeable affect. As the amount of alcohol is increased and the time between drinks shortened, the effects of the alcohol, such as slurred speech, impaired movements, senses, and judgment, become apparent. If a drinker is heavy, the alcohol is absorbed more slowly, and the effects of the alcohol occur more slowly than if the drinker is thin. If there is food in the stomach, the absorption rate of the alcohol is also slowed. Finally, each person is different and metabolizes the alcohol at a different rate. All of these factors work together to determine how quickly alcohol enters the blood stream.

Alcohol passes through the stomach and is absorbed through the walls of the intestines into the bloodstream. The blood carries the alcohol to the various organ systems of the body, where it is absorbed. Small amounts of the alcohol are processed by the kidneys and secreted in the urine. Small amounts are processed through the lungs and exhaled in the breath. If you have ever been close to someone who was drinking heavily, you probably have been able to smell the alcohol being exhaled. Most of the alcohol, however, is absorbed by the liver.

Heavy drinking of alcohol is associated with many health problems. Doctors have seen the devastating effects of excessive drinking on major organ systems of the human body. These effects accumulate over the years and can be fatal.

The bad effects of drinking alcohol do not only occur over a long period of time; there are short-term effects as well. Alcohol muddles the manner in which the brain works, making it difficult for the drinker to remember, think, pay attention, or learn. Just five drinks or more at one time affects a person's abstract thinking skills for almost a month, even if the person doesn't have another drink. Of course, if the person drinks more than five drinks, then abstract thinking is affected even more. What this means is that if a student drinks heavily on a weekend, his/her ability to analyze problems, compare concepts, and be creative will be impaired for a month. If he/she drinks every weekend, then he/she is never working up to his/her full potential. Once the student stops drinking, however, his/her abstract thinking returns to normal after a month.

This muddling of the brain is also the reason why alcohol contributes to accidents on the highway, at the workplace, or at home. People who are under the influence of alcohol cannot react as quickly because their brain activity is slowed by the alcohol. Therefore, they cannot safely operate vehicles and machines or sometimes even walk through their homes without hurting themselves. Alcohol-related traffic accidents are a major cause of death and injury for both those drinking and for innocent victims on the road.

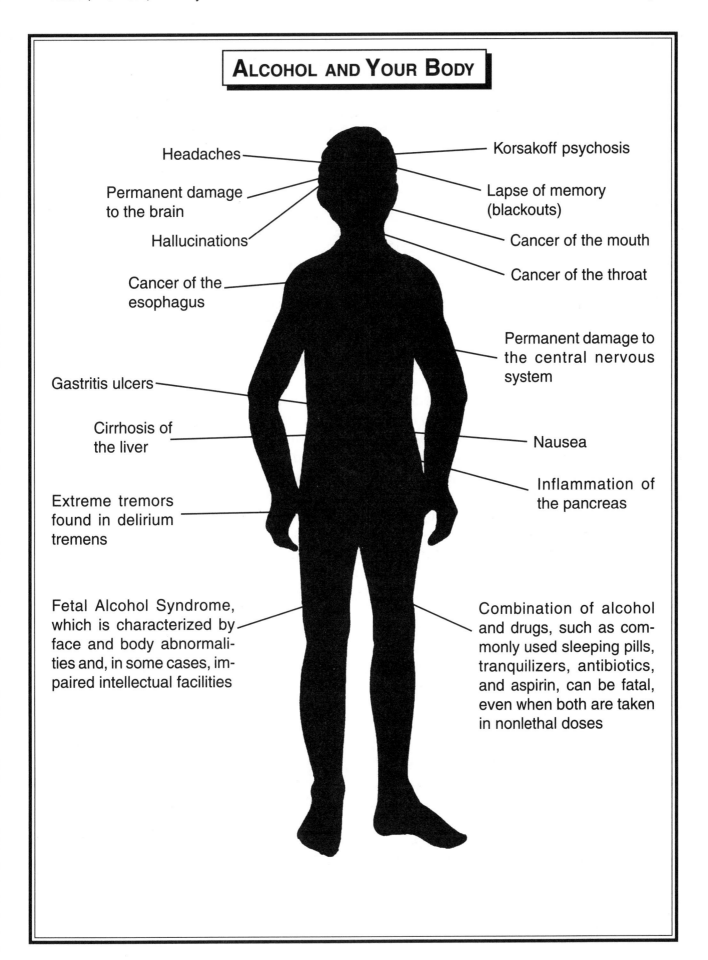

ALCOHOL AND YOUR BODY

Headaches

Permanent damage to the brain

Hallucinations

Cancer of the esophagus

Gastritis ulcers

Cirrhosis of the liver

Extreme tremors found in delirium tremens

Fetal Alcohol Syndrome, which is characterized by face and body abnormalities and, in some cases, impaired intellectual facilities

Korsakoff psychosis

Lapse of memory (blackouts)

Cancer of the mouth

Cancer of the throat

Permanent damage to the central nervous system

Nausea

Inflammation of the pancreas

Combination of alcohol and drugs, such as commonly used sleeping pills, tranquilizers, antibiotics, and aspirin, can be fatal, even when both are taken in nonlethal doses

Drugs

A word that causes a great deal of confusion is *drug*. Drugs can cure fevers, headaches, coughs, and even save our lives. If it weren't for drugs, many who are now in this classroom would not be alive. If you can, visit a very old cemetery and study the dates on old tombstones. You may be surprised to see the large number of children who died before they became adults. Many of the deaths were caused by epidemics and diseases that are no longer a threat due to the development of drugs. Drugs are an important part of our lives and our culture.

On the other hand, we hear the government is waging a war against drugs. We hear drugs can kill and can ruin lives. We hear drugs are illegal and the possession of drugs can send a person to jail for many years. The difference, of course, is that some drugs are developed to make us well. These drugs are called **medicines**, which are strictly regulated by the Federal Drug Administration, part of the United States government. Before a drug or medicine is approved for manufacture and distribution for use, it is tested for several years to be sure there are no **side effects** that could harm the user. Although these medicines are **legal** drugs and enable us to live long, happy, pain-free lives, we need to remember they are still drugs, and if not used properly, can be very dangerous.

Some of the most commonly used legal drugs are usually overlooked when people talk about drug use. Nicotine and alcohol are legal drugs, although they are only sold to adults. Nicotine is in cigarettes, cigars, pipe tobacco, and chewing tobacco. Alcohol is available in beer, wine, and liquor. Like all drugs, nicotine and alcohol affect the way our bodies work and can be the cause of health problems. These drugs are addictive.

Another class of drugs are **illegal drugs**. Illegal drugs are not tested or approved by the government. They are grown or manufactured and sold by criminals whose sole purpose is to make a profit. When someone buys an illegal drug, they really don't know what they are getting, and they don't know how weak or how powerful a dosage they are receiving. Poisonous chemicals or other foreign substances may be mixed in with the drug.

Most people take illegal drugs to feel euphoric, or "get high," but most illegal drugs are **addictive**, which means the user develops a compelling desire to use the drug. When one becomes addicted to a drug, there is a need to continually take the drug in order to feel normal. Drug addicts often create a **tolerance** for the drug and need to take more to get the same effect, but increasing the dosage in order to get the same effect can lead to an **overdose**. An overdose occurs when too strong a dose is taken and the user is injured, becomes sick, or dies.

Drugs can be classified in many ways but are often grouped into five categories: **stimulants**, **depressants**, **narcotics**, **hallucinogens**, and **inhalants**. The drugs in all of these categories have one thing in common: they are dangerous because they affect the natural rhythm and function of the body. They change the way the body and brain work. They may speed up or slow down the heart rate and blood pressure; reduce activity of the central nervous system; produce hallucinations, panic attacks, and psychotic effects; and cause the heart, kidneys, liver, lungs, or brain to shut down. Most drugs are addictive either physically or psychologically, and many can cause death.

DRUGS AND THEIR EFFECTS

CLASS	DRUGS	EFFECTS
Stimulants	Amphetamine Cocaine Crack	Increases alertness, heart rate, and blood pressure. Lowers fatigue, appetite, and causes sleeplessness. Can cause hallucinations and delusions. An overdose can cause death.
Depressants	Alcohol Tranquilizers Barbiturates	Reduces the activity of the central nervous system. Low doses reduce anxiety, but high doses can cause coma or death. An overdose can cause death.
Narcotics	Codeine Morphine Heroin Opium Methadone	Extracted from the opium poppy, their chemical by-products, or chemical compounds resembling the opiates in their actions. Narcotics decrease pain, provide a feeling of euphoria, and are highly addictive.
Hallucinogens	LSD PCP Mescaline Psilocybin Marijuana Hashish	Changes the way users see and hear. Sights and sounds are perceived in bizarre and often frightening ways. These drugs produce anxiety, panic attacks, psychotic effects, flashbacks, hallucinations, permanent brain damage, and death.
Inhalants	Paint thinner Model glue Gasoline Correction fluid Freon Aerosol spray	Causes headaches, hallucinations, nausea, disorientation, violent behavior, confusion, and memory loss. Causes decreased heart and respiratory function, and damage to kidneys, liver, bone marrow, and brain. Can cause death.

Name _____ Date _____

HE SAYS. YOU SAY.

You may have heard the saying, "The best defense is a good offense." What this means is that it is better to state your beliefs instead of explaining why you don't believe the way someone else does. You can do this more easily if you spend some time deciding what you believe and how your beliefs will control your actions. Once you do this, it is more difficult for others to persuade you to do something you really don't want to do. Here is an exercise that will give you an opportunity to think about what might happen and how you can respond.

Suppose you are at a party with no adults present and a friend comes up to you and offers you an illegal drug. Here are some of the things he might say. What would you say? Write your responses.

He Says	**You Say**
1. Everyone at the party is using this. Want to try some?	1._____ _____
2. Hey, this is expensive stuff, and you can have it for nothing.	2._____ _____
3. You're making too big a deal out of it. What is a little bit going to hurt?	3._____ _____
4. It won't hurt to try it just once.	4._____ _____
5. No one will find out.	5._____ _____
6. All the kids at school use it. Do you think you're better than everyone else?	6._____ _____
7. What's the matter, you afraid?	7._____ _____
8. I use it. Do you think I would use it if it could hurt you?	8._____ _____
9. Are you some kind of geek or weirdo?	9._____ _____
10. Do you think somebody would sell it if it could hurt you?	10._____ _____

Name _____ Date _____

SUBSTANCE ABUSE DISCUSSION QUESTIONS

Answer the following questions and be prepared to discuss them in class.

1. Describe what most people think of when they hear the word "alcoholic."

_____

_____

   Is their perception accurate? Why or why not? _____

_____

2. Describe what most people think of when they hear the word "junkie."

_____

_____

   Is their perception accurate? Why or why not? _____

_____

3. You are going to the prom with a boy you have always wanted to date. He picks you up in his parents' car and wants to go by his house so that his parents can see you both dressed up. While you are there, your date opens a bottle of beer and drinks it. What would you do? _____

_____

_____

4. Your eight-year-old sister has a friend visiting. When her friend's older brother comes to drive her home, his speech is slurred, and you smell alcohol on his breath. What would you do? _____

_____

_____

5. You are at your friend's house, and her parents aren't home. She offers you a marijuana cigarette and you refuse. She decides to have one anyway. What would you do?

_____

_____

_____

_____

Name_____ Date _____

SUBSTANCE ABUSE DISCUSSION QUESTIONS (CONTINUED)

6. You are looking in your younger brother's room for a calculator. In one of his desk drawers you find a package of cigarettes. What would you do? _____

_____

_____

7. You find out that one of your friends is not only using illegal drugs, but he is also selling them to elementary school students. What would you do? _____

_____

_____

8. Your father gets off work at 4:00, but he never gets home until 7:00. He always smells of smoke and alcohol and has trouble walking when he gets home. He has a few drinks and then goes to bed. You are afraid he might have a drinking problem. What would you do? _____

_____

_____

9. Your friend, Jim, has a drug problem, which he refuses to admit. His personality has changed, he is flunking most of his classes, and he has lost most of his friends. His parents are unaware of the drug problem. They only know Jim is having some problems. They invite you over and ask if you know what is bothering Jim. What would you do?

_____

_____

_____

10. You are invited to the party of the year. Everybody who is anybody will be there. You really want to go, but you learn there will be no adults at the party, and there will be alcohol and marijuana available. What would you do? _____

_____

_____

Name _____   Date _____

SUBSTANCE ABUSE DISCUSSION QUESTIONS (CONTINUED)

11. List five good reasons not to smoke:

    A. _____

    B. _____

    C. _____

    D. _____

    E. _____

12. List five good reasons not to take illegal drugs:

    A. _____

    B. _____

    C. _____

    D. _____

    E. _____

13. List five good reasons not to drink alcohol:

    A. _____

    B. _____

    C. _____

    D. _____

    E. _____

Name _____ Date _____

DESIGN A BOOKMARK

   Using the form shown below, design a bookmark intended to discourage substance abuse. Concentrate on the message. Your message should discourage someone from smoking, drinking, or using illegal drugs. What will you say, and how will you say it? You might look at commercials on television or advertisements in newspapers and magazines in order to see how professionals persuade the public. However, you should remember, this must be original. You should not copy a commercial or advertisement.

   Use any resources you like. You might want to include illustrations, designs, drawings, or pictures from magazines. You can use a computer or typewriter to create the bookmark or you might choose to write or print your message by hand. As a class, you can choose several different designs, make several copies of each, and present them to the school library for distribution.

Front	Back

Nutrition

Nutrition is the way that plants and animals take in food and use it for the growth and replacement of tissues. There are 50 **nutrients** in foods that can be divided into six groups: **proteins, fats, carbohydrates, water, vitamins**, and **minerals.** Humans need a certain amount of these nutrients each day for bodies to work properly and to stay healthy.

Proteins are made up of chains that contain many links called **amino acids**. There are twenty amino acids. Some are broken down to make energy for the body, and some are rearranged by the body into new proteins. The main job of protein is to build working body tissues, but proteins are also used to form parts of muscle, hair, skin, nails, connective tissue, and glands.

Carbohydrates can be divided into two categories: **simple carbohydrates** and **complex carbohydrates**. Simple carbohydrates are sugars, and complex carbohydrates are chains of sugars known as starches. For example, sucrose or table sugar is considered a simple carbohydrate. The starch found in bread, noodles, potatoes, or rice is considered a complex carbohydrate, since it is made up of chains of sugars. When we eat carbohydrates, they combine with oxygen and release energy so the body can function. Carbohydrates that have not been used up in energy are stored in the body and turned into fat.

Water makes up more than half of the human body. The body needs water to carry nutrients to cells, get rid of waste materials, circulate blood, and control body temperature. In fact, all bodily functions depend on the presence of water. A person's body loses water during urination, perspiration, and breathing. Water lost must be replaced frequently with water found in foods and drinks. In order to ensure one is getting enough water—two to three quarts a day—a person must drink several glasses of water each day. This must be increased on warm days when one is active.

Minerals are natural substances from the earth's crust. At least fourteen different minerals are necessary for human life. A balanced diet usually provides all the minerals a person needs. The body uses minerals in several ways. Some minerals, like calcium and phosphorus, build teeth and bones. Phosphorus also helps build nerve and brain tissue. Iron builds red blood cells. Some minerals control the activities of cells and organs. Calcium is needed for muscles to function properly. Because the heart is a muscle, calcium is necessary for the heartbeat. The liquid in blood vessels must have sodium and potassium so the body's tissues and cells can work properly. Tiny amounts of other minerals, called **trace elements**, are also needed. The trace elements include cobalt, copper, magnesium, manganese, zinc, and iodine. The body needs such small amounts of these minerals that it was once almost impossible for scientists to measure how much of them we need. But life cannot go on without these little traces of special minerals.

Vitamins are nutrients that are necessary for the body to stay healthy and alive. We must have vitamins in our diet because our bodies are not able to make them or only make them in insufficient amounts. Vitamins can be found in various foods, and each vitamin performs a different job in the body. Since one vitamin cannot do another vitamin's job, it is important to eat a variety of foods in order for the body to get all of the vitamins it needs. Unfortunately, when many think of vitamins, they simply think of pills and capsules instead of a well-balanced diet. Many believe that taking vitamin pills will make them stronger and healthier, but the truth is, vitamins can't make your muscles bigger, and they can't give you

Nutrition (continued)

more energy. They can only return health to people who have been sick because of a poor diet.

Vitamins are needed in only small amounts, because each molecule of a vitamin is used again and again—over a billion times a day. They aren't needed on a daily basis, because they can last a very long time. Also, vitamins are so common in everyday foods, that it is actually very difficult to not have enough. So, it is unlikely that you need to get any of your vitamins from a pill. In fact, taking large doses of certain vitamins can actually make you sick.

Today, there are thirteen known vitamins, which are divided into two classes: fat soluble and water soluble. Fat soluble vitamins dissolve in fat and oils and are stored in body fat, while water soluble vitamins dissolve in water. The fat soluble vitamins are A, D, E, and K. The water soluble vitamins are biotin, pantothenic acid, folic acid, Vitamin C, and the Vitamin B family—B1 (thiamine), B2 (riboflavin), B3 (niacin), B6 (pyridoxine), and B12 (cobalomine).

NUTRITION AND YOUR BODY

The nutrition process begins when food enters the mouth and is chewed until it becomes small bits. Saliva mixes with the food and breaks down the starches into dextrin and maltose.

Vitamins are vital for metabolism and to protect one's health. They help the formation of blood cells, hormones, nervous-system chemicals, and genetic material. The vegetable, fruit, and milk food groups all provide many vitamins.

Carbohydrates, the most abundant food sources of energy, are converted into simple sugars such as glucose. If the glucose is not used immediately, it is stored in the liver or muscles. The bread and cereal food group provide a great deal of one's carbohydrate intake.

Fats are converted into fatty acids and glycerol, which are either used immediately or stored in fat cells. Butter, oils, margarine, and sugars are major sources of fat.

Minerals, such as iron, calcium, and iodine are an important part of all cells and body fluids. The vegetable, fruit, and milk food groups are all important sources of minerals.

Protein, which is broken down into amino acid, is needed for growth and repair of tissues. The main job of protein is to build body tissue and to coordinate enzymes. The meat food group is a major source of protein, although the milk group and vegetables also provide protein.

Dietary fiber, a secondary category of complex carbohydrates, provides no nutrients, but is important to diets. Fiber consists of material in the food that is indigestible. It adds bulk in the stomach and intestines and provides more time for absorption of nutrients. The bread, rice, pasta, and cereal, and the vegetable and fruit food groups all provide fiber.

Name _____ Date _____

NUTRITION TRUE-FALSE TEST

Shown below are several statements. Some of the statements are true and some are false. If the statement is true, write "true" in the space before the statement. If the statement is false, look at the word in bold type. Could you replace the word in bold type with another word that would make the sentence correct? If so, write that word in the space before the statement.

_____ 1. Tiny amounts of minerals are called **trifling** elements.

_____ 2. The main job of **protein** is to build working body tissues.

_____ 3. Dietary fiber contains an indigestible material known as **cellulite**.

_____ 4. **Meat** is a good source of roughage.

_____ 5. A **calorie** is a unit of heat.

_____ 6. Milk is a **complete protein** food.

_____ 7. A **dietitian** is a scientist who works in the nutrition field.

_____ 8. **Carbohydrates** are made up of amino acids.

_____ 9. Calcium, iodine, and iron are all **minerals.**

_____ 10. **Simple carbohydrates** are sugars.

_____ 11. All bodily functions depend upon the presence of **water**.

_____ 12. **Vitamins** are natural substances from the earth's crust.

_____ 13. **Amino acids** are chains of sugars.

_____ 14. **Trace** vitamins are vitamins that dissolve in fat.

_____ 15. There are **twenty** amino acids.

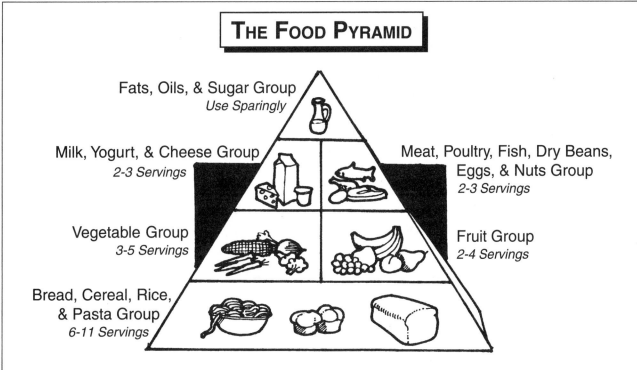

The Food Pyramid was created by the U.S. Department of Agriculture/U.S. Department of Health and Human Services as a guide to follow in order to maintain a healthy diet.

Breads, Cereals, Rice, & Pasta Group—*recommended 6 to 11 servings a day.*
Examples: One serving is equal to 1 slice bread; $\frac{1}{2}$ cup cooked rice, pasta, or cereal; 1 ounce cold cereal.

Vegetable Group—*recommended 3 to 5 servings a day.*
Examples: One serving is equal to $\frac{1}{2}$ cup chopped raw or cooked vegetables; 1 cup of leafy raw vegetables.

Fruit Group—*recommended 2 to 4 servings a day.*
Examples: One serving is equal to 1 piece of fruit or a melon wedge; $\frac{3}{4}$ cup juice; $\frac{1}{2}$ cup canned fruit; $\frac{1}{4}$ cup dried fruit.

Milk, Yogurt, & Cheese Group—*recommended 2 to 3 servings a day.*
Examples: One serving is equal to 1 cup milk or yogurt; $\frac{1}{2}$ to 2 ounces cheese.

Meat, Poultry, Fish, Dry Beans, Eggs, & Nuts Group—*recommended 2 to 3 servings a day.*
Examples: One serving is equal to $2\frac{1}{2}$ to 3 ounces of cooked lean meat, poultry, or fish; 1 to $1\frac{1}{2}$ cup cooked beans; 1 egg; 4 tablespoons peanut butter.

Fats, Oils, & Sugar—*recommended to be used sparingly.*
Examples: These are foods such as salad dressings, cream, butter, margarine, sugars, candies, sweet desserts, and soft drinks.

IDENTIFY THE FOOD GROUPS

Shown below are pictures of a number of foods. Decide in which of the six food groups each food should be included. Place the letter of the food group on the line above the food. The first is given as a sample.

A. Breads, Cereals, Rice, & Pasta Group
B. Vegetable Group
C. Fruit Group
D. Milk, Yogurt, & Cheese Group
E. Meat, Poultry, Fish, Dry Beans, Eggs, & Nuts Group
F. Fats, Oils, & Sugar Group

1. __C__

2. _____

3. _____

4. _____

5. _____

6. _____

7. _____

8. _____

9. _____

10. _____

11. _____

12. _____

13. _____

14. _____

15. _____

16. _____

17. _____

18. _____

19. _____

20. _____

21. _____

22. _____

23. _____

24 _____

Name _____ Date _____

THE ABCs OF NUTRITION

Fill in the blank with the appropriate word or phrase. The answer for the letter "X" is given as an example.

A is for _____ , which is an eating disorder that usually occurs in adolescent girls. A patient with this psychological disorder becomes so obsessed with her weight that she reduces food intake to starvation levels.

B is for _____ , which is an eating disorder. A patient may consume a lot of food at meals and then induce vomiting or take laxatives so the food does not have a chance to digest.

C is for _____ , which includes sugars, starches, celluloses, and gums and serves as a major energy source in the diet of animals.

D is for _____ , the food group containing milk, cheese, butter, and yogurt.

E is for _____ _____ , a product containing the highest amount of saturated fat and cholesterol of any food.

F is for _____ , the indigestible part of foods. Whole grains, vegetables, fruits, and legumes are all good sources.

G is for _____ , which includes foods such as breads and cereals.

H is for _____ _____ , which may be avoided by reducing the amount of fat and cholesterol you consume and increasing your fiber intake.

I is for _____ , which is a mineral. If a person does not receive this substance in proper amounts, anemia may develop.

J is for _____ _____ , which are foods high in calories but low in nutritional value.

K is for _____ , which are the pair of organs responsible for maintaining proper water and electrolyte balance and filtering the blood of metabolic wastes.

L is for _____ _____ , which is sometimes called "bad" cholesterol because pieces easily become stuck along blood vessel walls.

M is for _____ , which is the process in which some substances are broken down to yield energy while other substances are synthesized.

49

Name _____ Date _____

THE ABCs OF NUTRITION (CONTINUED)

N is for _____ , which is a component of the Vitamin B complex found in meat, wheat germ, dairy products, and yeast.

O is for _____ , which is a disease in which the bones become extremely porous, are easily fractured, and are slow to heal. It often leads to curvature of the spine.

P is for _____ , which is made up of links of amino acids. Its main function is to build working body tissue.

Q is for _____ , which one must meet daily in the consumption of vitamins and minerals.

R is for _____ , which stands for the recommended daily allowance of nutrients.

S is for _____ , which is the type of fat found mainly in meat and dairy products.

T is for _____ _____ , which may occur as a result of eating too many sweets and failing to brush regularly.

U is for _____ , which is fat found in vegetables.

V is for _____ , a person who does not consume meat or animal products.

W is for _____ , the substance that makes up more than half of the human body.

X is for Xylem , the supporting and water-conducting tissue of vascular plants.

Y is for _____ , a custard-like dairy product that may also be eaten frozen.

Z is for _____ , which is a trace mineral.

HEALTH NOTEBOOK   Name _____ Date _____

FOOD DIARY

Keep a record of all of the food, including snacks, you eat during the week. For each food you eat, list it under the appropriate food group. For example, if you ate a banana for breakfast on Sunday, you would write "banana" opposite Sunday under the fruit category.

	GRAINS	VEGETABLES	FRUIT	MEAT	MILK	FATS
Sunday						
Monday						
Tuesday						
Wednesday						
Thursday						
Friday						
Saturday						

HEALTH NOTEBOOK   Name _____ Date _____

EVALUATING YOUR DIET

The Food Pyramid, created by the U.S. Department of Agriculture/ U.S. Department of Health and Human Services, illustrates that in order to maintain a healthy diet, a person should consume the recommended number of servings in the following food groups each day:

Breads, Cereals, Rice, & Pasta Group—*recommended 6 to 11 servings per day.*
Vegetable Group—*recommended 3 to 5 servings a day.*
Fruit Group—*recommended 2 to 4 servings a day.*
Milk, Yogurt, & Cheese Group—*recommended 2 to 3 servings a day .*
Meat, Poultry, Fish, Dry Beans, Eggs, & Nuts Group—*recommended 2 to 3 servings a day.*
Fats, Oils, and Sugar—*recommended used sparingly.*

When you kept a food diary for one week, did you meet these recommended guidelines? Using the food diary, answer the following questions.

1. Monday: Estimate the number of servings for each food group for

    bread ____   vegetable ____   fruit ____   milk ____   meat ____   oils ____
2. Tuesday: Estimate the number of servings for each food group for

    bread ____   vegetable ____   fruit ____   milk ____   meat ____   oils ____
3. Wednesday: Estimate the number of servings for each food group for

    bread ____   vegetable ____   fruit ____   milk ____   meat ____   oils ____
4. Thursday: Estimate the number of servings for each food group for

    bread ____   vegetable ____   fruit ____   milk ____   meat ____   oils ____
5. Friday: Estimate the number of servings for each food group for

    bread ____   vegetable ____   fruit ____   milk ____   meat ____   oils ____
6. Saturday: Estimate the number of servings for each food group for

    bread ____   vegetable ____   fruit ____   milk ____   meat ____   oils ____
7. Sunday: Estimate the number of servings for each food group for

    bread ____   vegetable ____   fruit ____   milk ____   meat ____   oils ____
8. Over the weekly period, what food groups did you have that exceeded the recommended daily number of servings? _____

9. Over the weekly period, what food groups failed to meet the recommended daily number of servings? _____

10. What changes could you make in order to make your diet healthier?

_____

_____

HEALTH NOTEBOOK   Name _____   Date _____

SCHOOL LUNCH DIARY

Keep a record of the school lunch menu for one week. List each food under the appropriate food group. For example, if a hamburger is served on Monday, you would write "hamburger" opposite Monday under the meat category and "bun" under the grains category.

Day	Grains	Vegetables	Fruit	Meat	Milk	Fats
Monday						
Tuesday						
Wednesday						
Thursday						
Friday						

1. Even though this is just one meal during the day, what general conclusions can you draw concerning the school lunch program? _____

2. Ask your teacher, a cook, or the school principal the purpose of the school lunch program. Write the purpose here. _____

3. Do you feel the school is meeting its purpose? _____

Name _____ Date _____

PLANNING A NUTRITIOUS MENU

How inexpensively can you plan a nutritious menu for a family? Keeping the food pyramid in mind, plan the meals for one day for a family of four. While your primary goal is to make the meals nutritious, try to spend as little money as possible. Also, keep the amount of fat as low as possible. Use the following steps in order to complete the assignment.

STEPS

1. Write the menus in the spaces below.
2. Beneath the menus, make a list of the ingredients necessary to fix the meals.
3. Go to the supermarket and find items you need to prepare the meals. Write the food group the product represents and the price of the item in the space provided.

Breakfast

Lunch

Dinner

Snacks

Item	Food Group	Total Fat	Cost
1. _____	_____	_____	_____
2. _____	_____	_____	_____
3. _____	_____	_____	_____
4. _____	_____	_____	_____
5. _____	_____	_____	_____
6. _____	_____	_____	_____
7. _____	_____	_____	_____
8. _____	_____	_____	_____
9. _____	_____	_____	_____
10. _____	_____	_____	_____
11. _____	_____	_____	_____
12. _____	_____	_____	_____
13. _____	_____	_____	_____
14. _____	_____	_____	_____
		Total Cost	_____

Name _____ Date _____

NUTRITION IN FAST FOODS

Just how nutritious is the fast food you buy? Listed below are some food items sold at many fast food chains. Go to several fast food restaurants and ask about the nutritional content of the items listed and fill in the chart. Discuss your findings. For example, are there significant differences between an item in one restaurant and a similar one in another restaurant? Were they prepared differently, or do they have different ingredients?

ITEM	CALORIES	PROTEIN	CARBS.	FATS	SODIUM
Quarter-pound Hamburger					
1.					
2.					
Bacon Cheeseburger					
1.					
2.					
Fish Fillet Sandwich					
1.					
2.					
Breakfast Egg Sandwich					
1.					
2.					
French Fries					
1.					
2.					
Chocolate Shake					
1.					
2.					
Banana Split					
1.					
2.					
Regular Beef Taco					
1.					
2.					
Thick Crust Pepperoni Pizza					
1.					
2.					
Fried Chicken Dinner (3 pieces chicken)					
1.					
2.					

On a separate sheet of paper, write a two page essay entitled "Nutrition and Fast Food Restaurants." The essay will explain your thoughts, feelings, and opinions and will be based on what you and your classmates have discovered by filling in the chart shown above.

UNDERSTANDING FOOD LABELS

Under federal regulations, most foods have labels that provide nutritional information. A nutritional label, entitled "Nutritional Facts," lists the serving size, calories per serving, the percentage of RDA (U.S .Recommended Daily Allowance) of certain nutrients for people over four, the ingredients, and a product date.

Serving Sizes are based on amounts people actually eat and are uniform across product lines.

Calories From Fat are important, since it is recommended that people get no more than 30 percent of their calories from fat.

(%) Daily Value enables one to easily determine if a product is high or low in a nutrient. The Daily Value is based on a general diet.

The **Daily Values,** shown at the bottom of the nutrition label, list the recommended *minimum amounts* of some nutrients and food elements such as carbohydrates and fiber. They also show recommended *maximum amounts* for others, such as fat, saturated fat, cholesterol, and sodium.

There are two Daily Value columns, since nutrient needs differ with the amount of calories you eat. The label provides Daily Values for both a 2,000-calorie diet and a 2,500-calorie diet.

The label also tells the number of **calories per gram of fat, carbohydrate, and protein**.

The **ingredients** found in the product are listed using common names. Some common names for sugars include corn syrup, fructose, honey, mannitol, molasses, sorbitol, and sucrose. Some common names for fats include coconut oil, butter, lard, hydrogenated oil, palm oil, and other oils.

The ingredients are listed in descending order by weight. This means that the food product contains more of whatever is listed first. In the example on the right, there is more long grain parboiled rice than any other ingredient.

Nutrition Facts

Serving Size 1/2 cup (114 g)
Servings Per Container 4

Amount Per Serving

Calories 70 Calories From Fat 20

		% Daily Value*
Total Fat	3g	5%
Saturated Fat	0g	0%
Cholesterol	0mg	0%
Sodium	300mg	14%
Total Carbohydrate	13g	4%
Dietary Fiber	3g	16%
Sugars	3g	
Protein	3g	

Vitamin A	80%
Vitamin C	60%
Calcium	4%
Iron	4%

* Percent Daily Values are based on a 2,000 calorie diet. Your daily values may be higher or lower, depending on your calorie needs:

		Calories	2,000	2,500
Total Fat	Less than		65g	80g
Sat Fat	Less than		20g	25g
Cholesterol	Less than		300mg	300mg
Sodium	Less than		2,400mg	2,400mg
Total Carbohydrate			300g	375g
Fiber			25g	30g

Calories per gram:
Fat 9 • Carbohydrate 5 • Protein 4

INGREDIENTS: LONG GRAIN PARBOILED RICE ENRICHED WITH FERRIC ORTHO PHOSPHATE (IRON) AND THIAMINE MONONITRATE (THIAMINE); CHEESE* (CHEDDAR CHEESE, MILK, SALT, CULTURES, AND ENZYMES); ROMANO MADE FROM COW'S MILK (MILK, SALT, CULTURES AND ENZYMES), AND PARMESAN CHEESE (MILK, SALT, CULTURES, AND ENZYMES); MODIFIED CORNSTARCH; PARTIALLY HYDROGENATED SOYBEAN AND/OR COTTONSEED OIL; WHEY; VEGETABLES* (BROCCOLI, ONION, PARSLEY, CABBAGE, PEAS); BUTTERMILK*; HYDROLYZED SOY/WHEAT GLUTEN PROTEIN; SALT; NONFAT MILK*; SODIUM PHOSPHATE; LACTIC ACID; XANTHAN GUM; SPICES; AUTOLYZED YEAST EXTRACT; NATURAL FLAVOR; ANNATTO (COLOR); LECITHIN; MONO AND DIGLYCERIDES; SODIUM BISULFITE (TO PRESERVE FRESHNESS). * DRIED.

Name_____ Date_____

INTERPRETING FOOD LABELS

A

Nutrition Facts

Serving Size 3/4 cup (27g)
Servings Per Container 22

Amount Per Serving

Calories 100   Calories From Fat 0
                              % Daily Value*

Total Fat 0g	0%
Saturated Fat 0g	0%
Cholesterol 0 mg	0%
Sodium 135 mg	6%
Total Carbohydrate 25g	8%
Dietary Fiber 0g	0%
Sugars 16g	
Protein 1g	

Vitamin A 0%   Vitamin C 0%
Calcium 0%   Iron 2%
 * Percent Daily Values are based on a 2,000 calorie diet. Your daily values may be higher or lower, depending on your calorie needs:

Fat 9 • Carbohydrate 4 • Protein 4

INGREDIENTS: Sugar, brown sugar, corn syrup, popped popcorn, salt, natural and artificial butter-scotch/caramel flavor, corn oil*, lecithin (an emulsifier)* natural butter flavor, natural artificial honey flavor.
*Adds trivial amount of fat

B

Nutrition Facts

Serving Size 1/2 cup (120mL)
Servings Per Container 2.5

Amount Per Serving

Calories 70   Calories From Fat 20
                              % Daily Value*

Total Fat 2g	3%
Saturated Fat 1g	5%
Cholesterol 15mg	5%
Sodium 980mg	41%
Total Carbohydrate 9g	3%
Dietary Fiber 1g	4%
Sugars 1g	
Protein 3g	

Vitamin A 6%   Vitamin C 0%
Calcium 2%   Iron 4%
 * Percent Daily Values are based on a 2,000 calorie diet. Your daily values may be higher or lower, depending on your calorie needs:

Fat 9 • Carbohydrate 4 • Protein 4

INGREDIENTS: Chicken Stock, enriched egg noodles (wheat floor, egg solids, niacin, ferrous sulfate, thiamine mononitrate, riboflavin) cooked chicken meat, water, contains less than 2% of the following ingredients: salt, chicken fat, cornstarch, cooked mechanically separated chicken, monosodium glutamate, onion powder, yeast extract, spice extract, sodium phosphates, modified food starch, soy protein isolate, beta carotene for color, chicken flavor (contains chicken stock, chicken powder, chicken fat), dehydrated garlic flavoring, and citric acid.

C

Nutrition Facts

Serving Size 1/12 pkg. (43g)
Servings Per Container 12

Amount Per Serving

Calories 250   Calories From Fat 100
                              % Daily Value*

Total Fat 11g	17%
Saturated Fat 3g	14%
Polyunsaturated 4g	
monounsaturated 4g	
Cholesterol 55mg	18%
Sodium 410 mg	17%
Total Carbohydrate 34g	11%
Dietary Fiber 1g	3%
Sugars 20g	
Protein 3g	

Calcium 2%   Iron   6%
Thiamin 6%   Riboflavin 8%
Niacin   2%
Not a significant source of vitamin A and C.
 * Percent Daily Values are based on a 2,000 calorie diet. Your daily values may be higher or lower, depending on your calorie needs:

Fat 9 • Carbohydrate 4 • Protein 4

INGREDIENTS: Sugar, enriched flour bleached (wheat flour, niacin, iron thiamin mononitrate, riboflavin) partially hydrogenated soybean and cottonseed oil, dextrose, leavening (baking soda, sodium aluminum phosphate, dicalcium phosphate, monocalcium phosphate, aluminum sulfate), cocoa processed with alkali, wheat starch, modified corn starch, whey, salt, corn starch, cellulose gum, mono and diglycerides, artificial flavor.

Shown above are the nutrition labels for three different food products.

1. Based on the label, what product do you think label A is from? _____

2. Based on the label, what product do you think label B is from? _____

3. Based on the label, what product do you think label C is from? _____

4. What is the largest ingredient in product A? _____

5. What is the largest ingredient in product B? _____

6. What is the largest ingredient in product C? _____

7. What is the second largest ingredient in product A? _____

8. What is the second largest ingredient in product B? _____

9. What is the second largest ingredient in product C? _____

Name _____ Date _____

INTERPRETING FOOD LABELS (CONTINUED)

10. If you were on a low-salt diet, which *one* of the above products would be the worst for you to eat? _____

11. Which product has the least number of ingredients? _____

12. If you were trying to lose weight, which *one* of the above products would be the best to avoid? _____

13. If you have atherosclerosis (a buildup of fatty material on the inner lining of an arterial wall), which one of these products is the best to avoid? _____

14. Which product has the *highest* percentage of RDA for vitamin A? _____

15. Which product has the *highest* percentage of RDA for iron? _____

16. Which product has the *lowest* percentage of RDA for calcium? _____

17. Which product has the *highest* percentage of RDA for thiamin? _____

18. Which product has the *highest* percentage of RDA for riboflavin? _____

19. Which product has the *highest* percentage of RDA for niacin? _____

20. Which product has the *highest* number of calories from fat? _____

21. Which product has the *highest* total of carbohydrates? _____

22. Which product has the *highest* amount of sugar? _____

23. Which product has the *lowest* amount of protein? _____

24. Which product has the *lowest* amount of fiber? _____

25. Which product seems to be the most "natural"? _____

26. Why is it important to have food labels?

_____

_____

_____

_____

_____

27. If you were compelled to exist on only one of these products for an extended period of time, which would you choose? Why?

_____

_____

_____

_____

_____

HEALTH NOTEBOOK   Name _____ Date _____

WEIGHT CONTROL

Someone who is overweight is said to be **obese**. Here are just a few of the problems we know that are caused by obesity: cardiovascular disease, hypertension (high blood pressure), adult-onset diabetes (Type II), osteoarthritis, sleep apnea, and female infertility. This is not a complete list, and more health problems caused by obesity are being discovered each year.

While everyone can understand it is not healthy to be very overweight or very underweight, how can one determine if they are at their correct weight? One way is to calculate your **Body Mass Index**. The **BMI** is a ratio between weight and height and is used to determine your nutritional status. Your BMI is a quick way of determining if you are too heavy or too thin for your height. Here is the formula for determining your BMI:

Step One: Multiply your weight in pounds by 703.
Step Two: Twice divide the result by your height in inches.

Example: You are five feet tall (60 inches) and weigh 140 pounds; find your BMI.
Step One: Weight (140) x 703 = 98,420
Step Two: 98,420 ÷ 60 ÷ 60 = 27.34

So your BMI is 27.34. What exactly does that mean? The ideal, average, acceptable range is between 20 and 25. Those with a BMI higher or lower than this range are at risk for health problems.

BMI	WEIGHT	RISK FACTOR
Below 16	Gaunt	Cause for Concern
17–20	Thin	Low
20–25	Average	Low
25–27	Slightly Overweight	Low to Moderate
27–30	Moderately Overweight	Moderately High
30–35	Severely Overweight	High
35–40	Obese	Very High
+40	Morbidly Obese	Extremely High

Figuring Your BMI

What is your BMI? Figure your BMI below, and then check the chart above to see if your weight is normal, high, or low.

What is your weight? (W) _____   What is your height in inches? (H) _____

Step One: (W) _____ X 703 = _____
Step Two: _____ ÷ (H) _____ ÷ (H) _____ = _____

The BMI is helpful for most adults, but it is less helpful for athletes or body builders who have a lot of muscle and are very heavy but are not fat. It is also not very helpful for pregnant women, growing children, or frail, elderly people.

Name _____ Date _____

WEIGHT REDUCTION

While most young people are not overweight, as people grow older, they tend to become less active and gain weight. This problem is particularly obvious in the United States. U.S. citizens are among the most overweight people in the world. Why do you suppose this is? The ancestors of most U.S. citizens came from other countries. Genetically, our citizens should be similar to those who live in the countries from which our ancestors came.

1. List five reasons you think U.S. citizens may be more obese than those from other countries.

    a. _____

    b. _____

    c. _____

    d. _____

    e. _____

2. List four causes of obesity.

    a. _____

    b. _____

    c. _____

    d. _____

3. List five diseases or health problems associated with obesity or being overweight.

    a. _____

    b. _____

    c. _____

    d. _____

    e. _____

4. List ten healthy ways to lose weight permanently.

    a. _____

    b. _____

    c. _____

    d. _____

    e. _____

    f. _____

    g. _____

    h. _____

    i. _____

    j. _____

Mental and Emotional Health

Mental health not only affects emotions, it can also affect one's physical health.

- People with severe depression are more likely to commit suicide.
- People who are optimistic have fewer chronic diseases than those who are pessimistic.
- People with an angry or unfriendly personality have a higher risk of heart attack.
- Unmarried people and those without friends have a higher death rate.
- People under stress who withdraw into themselves rather than socialize have a greater risk of cancer and suicide.

Stress and anxiety occur whenever a person is angry or afraid. Muscles are tensed, and hormones, such as adrenaline, are produced so that a person is able to fight or run away. When a person is experiencing stress, the body's natural resistance to illness is lowered. This can lead to headaches, indigestion, sleeping problems, ulcers, heart disease, and high blood pressure.

What can cause stress in a young person? The most stressful events include the death of a parent, brother, sister, grandparent, or other close relative. If parents separate, divorce, remarry, lose their jobs, or become ill, a young person may experience stress. Even the birth of a brother or sister can be a stressful event. These are only the major events that cause stress. Going out on a date, giving a speech, taking a test, and thousands of other activities may also cause stress.

People deal with stress in different ways. Some people listen to soothing music or sing. Others relieve their stress with laughter. They watch and laugh at a funny movie or television show rather than dwell on their negative thoughts. Relaxation is another popular way to relieve stress. So is helping others. When a person is concentrating on helping others, there is less time to think about his/her own problems.

DEALING WITH STRESS

Feeling sad? You're not unusual. Everyone is sad from time to time. Feeling sad or unhappy is especially common in teenagers. Perhaps you lost a relative, friend, or pet. Maybe your parents are getting a divorce or you are moving to a new town. Maybe your feelings have been hurt because people have teased you. Or you might not like the way you look or how well you do in school or in sports. These are all common reasons people feel sad. Fortunately, when a person is sad, it doesn't last very long. If your sadness lasts for more than a few days, it may mean you have a more serious problem called **depression**.

A person who is depressed often feels worthless, lonely, unloved, and that life is not worth living. While occasional thoughts such as these are nothing to be worried about, if you have a depression or sadness that will not go away, it is important to talk to an adult about it. You could talk to a parent, relative, friend, teacher, counselor, coach, minister, or doctor. There is always someone to talk to and someone who can help.

Those who do not seek help sometimes consider suicide. Suicide is the ninth leading cause of death in the United States and the second leading cause of death among teenagers and young adults. It is also a leading cause of death among children. Most people who consider suicide give clues that they intend to commit suicide and can be helped if the people around them are able to understand the signs and provide help. Some of the clues or signs that a person is considering suicide include:

- Talking or writing about suicide.
- Withdrawing from family and friends.
- Putting personal affairs in order.
- Giving away personal possessions.
- Loss of interest in usual activities.
- Talking about getting even with people.
- Losing interest in personal appearance and hygiene.
- Change in personality or in eating or sleeping habits.
- Difficulty in getting along with peers.
- Feelings of hopelessness, helplessness, and low self-worth.
- Increasing use of drugs or alcohol.

If a friend exhibits any of these signs, you should take them seriously and share your concerns with an adult who can help him/her, even if you promised not to tell anyone. Stay with the person who shows signs of suicidal behavior until a trusted adult arrives who is able to handle the situation. Remember, this is a very serious situation and is not something you can handle yourself. In fact, the adult you confide in will not be able to deal with the problem either. He or she will need to arrange for the person considering suicide to seek professional help.

HEALTH NOTEBOOK   Name _____ Date _____

A SUPPORT NETWORK

It is important to have a support network of people you can call on to help you when you are in trouble. Complete the following form of your support network. Put the form in your medical notebook where it will be available when needed.

Family Members

Name _____   Phone Number _____

Name _____   Phone Number _____

Friends

Name _____   Phone Number _____

Name _____   Phone Number _____

Non-family Adult

Name _____   Phone Number _____

Adult at School

Name _____   Phone Number _____

Member of Church

Name _____   Phone Number _____

Community Resources

Almost every community has resources that are available for someone who is depressed or unhappy. There may be a mental health clinic, a suicide hotline, or some other organization or person who is available to help those who are depressed. How about your community? Write their names and phone numbers in the spaces below.

Name _____   Phone Number _____

Name _____   Phone Number _____

Name _____   Phone Number _____

Name _____   Phone Number _____

Name _____ Date _____

HANDLING STRESS AND DEPRESSION

Respond to the following situations.

1. Ahmad, your friend, is unhappy because he was not elected class president. Things get worse when he is kicked off the basketball team. He tells you that nothing ever goes right for him, and he would be better off dead. What would you do?

_____

_____

2. You find a note that leads you to believe that Janet, your cousin, might be considering suicide. When you tell your father, he says, "Don't worry. People who talk about suicide never do it." What would you do?

_____

_____

3. You are concerned about a friend's mental health. She has become irritable, withdrawn, no longer cares about her appearance, and has given her younger sister her stereo and all of her favorite CDs. You decide to talk to her, but when you do, she seems strangely calm and at peace with the world. Should you still be concerned?

_____

_____

4. You are visiting a friend in a hospital after he has tried to kill himself. What should you say to him?

_____

_____

5. One of your friends calls you and says that he is going to kill himself. It is late and you are tired. What would you do?

_____

_____

6. One of your friends tells you that another friend, Carmen, is considering suicide. You have studied mental health in school and know you could talk her out of it, and people would consider you a hero. What should you do?

_____

_____

7. Bill has just moved into your town. He has no friends and the other students pick on him. He is sad and lonely and spends a lot of time talking about "getting even" with those who have made fun of him. You are worried, so you talk to him. He says not to worry. He wouldn't do anything to hurt himself. Should you be concerned?

_____

_____

HEALTH NOTEBOOK   Name _____ Date _____

REST AND SLEEPING

Rest is an important factor in your health. Inadequate rest causes bodies to function inefficiently. Thinking is difficult and skills involving movements are impaired. If a person does not get adequate rest, the body becomes worn out, making a person more susceptible to illness. How well do you sleep? To answer this question, you should make a record of one night's sleep. Use the form below.

Sleep Record

Name _____

Date _____ Day of the Week _____

1. Time you went to bed. _____

2. How long did it take you to fall asleep? _____

3. Was it difficult for you to fall asleep? _____

4. How many times did you awaken during the night? _____

5. How long did you sleep? _____

6. What time did you wake up? _____

7. Were you rested when you awoke? _____

8. What time did you get out of bed? _____

9. Describe your physical state when you went to bed. Were you relaxed or tense?

_____

_____

10. Describe your mental state when you went to bed. Were you relaxed or tense?

_____

_____

11. Was your bedroom conducive to rest? Was it quiet? Was it dark? Was there anything that might have interfered with your sleep?

_____

_____

12. How would you rate your night's sleep? Was it excellent, fair, or poor?

_____

13. What steps should you take in order to improve the quality of your sleep?

_____

_____

_____

_____

Name _____ Date _____

Consumer Health
HEALTH CARE FACILITIES IN MY COMMUNITY

Your community most likely has many different kinds of health care facilities. But do you know where they are all located and the purpose of each facility? Make a list of all of the health care facilities in your community. Your list should include hospitals, clinics, private health organizations, nursing homes, etc. Describe each facility and its function.

Facility	Address	Purpose
1.		
2.		
3.		
4.		
5.		
6.		
7.		
8.		
9.		
10.		
11.		
12.		
13.		
14.		
15.		
16.		
17.		
18.		

Name _____   Date _____

HEALTH CARE WORKERS

Write the correct health care worker on the blank next to the corresponding description of the health care specialty.

Health Care Worker   **Deals With**

1. _____ Diseases of the immune system

2. _____ Coronary artery disease; heart disease

3. _____ Treats mental illnesses

4. _____ Examines and tests eyes for visual defects

5. _____ Administration of anesthesia (for example, surgery)

6. _____ Care and treatment of the foot

7. _____ Pregnancy, labor, childbirth

8. _____ Treats problems of the skin

9. _____ Treatment of diseases in adults

10. _____ Female reproductive system

11. _____ General care of teeth and oral cavity

12. _____ Use of material to rebuild tissues

13. _____ Diseases and conditions of the aged

14. _____ Uses manipulation and adjustment to treat disease

15. _____ Study of tissues and the essential nature of disease

16. _____ Allergic conditions

17. _____ Childhood diseases and conditions

18. _____ General health and medical care

19. _____ Use of X-rays

20. _____ Treats problems of the nervous system

21. _____ Treats diseases by surgery

22. _____ Performs surgery on bones, joints, and muscles

23. _____ Teeth alignment, malocclusion

Allergist	**Immunologist**	**Pediatrician**
Anesthesiologist	**Internist**	**Plastic surgeon**
Cardiologist	**Neurologist**	**Podiatrist**
Chiropractor	**Obstetrician**	**Primary care physician**
Dentist	**Optometrist**	**Psychologist**
Dermatologist	**Orthodontist**	**Radiologist**
Geriatrician	**Orthopedist**	**Surgeon**
Gynecologist	**Pathologist**	

HEALTH NOTEBOOK   Name _____ Date _____

DOCTOR VISIT CHECKLIST

A doctor's appointment can be more beneficial if you prepare for the visit. Make a photocopy of this form to keep in your health notebook. The next time you or one of your family members has a doctor's appointment, fill out the checklist before the appointment, and take the form to your appointment.

Before the visit:

- When you make the appointment, tell the receptionist why you are making the appointment so she can schedule the right amount of time.
- If this is your first visit with this doctor, prepare your medical history, including chronic illnesses, operations, hospitalizations, allergies, and other physical problems.
- Make a list of prescription and over-the counter medications you are taking. (Form shown on next page.)
- Set aside a pen or a pencil to take to the visit.
- Write down your problem and the symptoms you are experiencing.
- Write down specific questions you want answered. Leave space to write down answers.

During the visit:

- Explain your problem, describe your symptoms, and relate past experiences you might have had with the same problem. Explain how you have tried to treat the problem.
- Ask questions.

Record the following:

- Temperature: _____   Blood pressure: _____ / _____

- Diagnosis (What the doctor says is wrong): _____

  _____

- Prognosis (What could happen because of your problem): _____

  _____

- What the doctor will do: _____

  _____

- What you can do at home: _____

  _____

HEALTH NOTEBOOK   Name _____ Date _____

DOCTOR VISIT CHECKLIST (CONTINUED)

Drugs, treatments and tests

- • Name: _____

- • Purpose: _____

- • Costs: _____

- • Risks: _____

- • Alternatives: _____

- • What if I do nothing? _____

  _____

- • (For drugs) How do I take this? _____

  _____

- • (For tests) How do I prepare? _____

  _____

At the end of the visit

- • Ask if a follow-up appointment is necessary.
- • If you have or will take tests, ask how and when you can get the results.
- • As a result of the treatment, what should I expect?
- • Ask if there are danger signs you should look for.

Medication Record

Name_____

Medicine	Dosage	Date Prescribed	Prescribing Doctor

Name_____ Date _____

COMPARE DIFFERENT MEDICATIONS

Everyone is a consumer. A consumer is a person who purchases and uses products and services. Some people estimate that approximately one-half of every dollar we spend is spent on health products and services. Obviously, it is important that we be wise consumers and learn all we can about the health products and services we intend to purchase. We must examine advertisements, analyze commercials, and carefully compare products and services in order to decide which are good for us and which are harmful or useless. Unfortunately, this is not easy. Since so much money is spent on health products and services, there is a great deal of exaggeration and fraud.

We are fortunate in the United States to have the opportunity to choose among many different brands of products. On the other hand, such a large selection of brands makes it difficult to make correct choices. The following exercise will give you an opportunity to compare similar products and to choose which is better. Go to the drug store and compare two different brands of each of the following products. Fill out the form below. You may want to ask the advice of the pharmacist.

Type	Brand #1	Price	Main Ingredients	Brand #2	Price	Main Ingredients
Aspirin						
Antacid						
Cough Syrup						
Cold Medicine						
Nasal Spray						

What, if anything, did you learn from comparing products? _____

_____

ORGAN DONATION

Scientists and physicians wondered for centuries whether it would ever be possible to replace diseased or damaged organs in humans with healthy organs from those who were killed or had died. Scientists conducted organ transplant experiments with animals and even with humans, but the results were always unsuccessful. It wasn't until the middle of the twentieth century, when researchers gained a greater understanding of the human immune system and were able to develop drugs to suppress the immune system, that there was any success in this field. Today, cornea, bone, cartilage, bone marrow, skin, heart, kidney, liver, pancreas, and lung transplants are common throughout the country and are no longer considered experimental. A single donor could donate as many as 25 organs and tissues.

There are actually two types of **organ donors**. **Living donors** can donate blood, and in certain cases, they may also donate bone marrow, a kidney, part of a lung, or part of a liver to a close family member. The other kind of donor is a person in good health who has died suddenly, often as a result of an accident. In many cases, the patient is **brain dead**, which means the function of the brain has permanently stopped, and there is no possibility that the patient can ever recover. Often when this occurs, the patient is put on life-support machines that enable the heart and lungs to continue to function even though the brain is not functioning and the patient cannot recover. If a patient who is brain dead had signed a donor card prior to his/her accident, and if the family gives permission, a transplant team is called to remove certain organs and tissues that may be transplanted in other patients. A donor who is recently deceased may donate his/her bone, eyes, heart, kidneys, liver, lungs, pancreas, skin, arteries and veins, heart valves, and cartilage.

Preservation times of organs

Corneas	10 days	Heart/Lung	5 hours
Bone	5 years or more	Liver	18 hours
Bone Marrow	varies	Lung	5 hours
Kidney	72 hours	Pancreas	20 hours
Heart	5 hours	Skin	5 years or more
Heart Valves	5 years or more		

People who are 18 years old or older and are of sound mind can express their wish to become donors by signing organ and tissue donor cards, keeping those cards with them, and telling their families that they wish to donate. When people apply for or renew their driver's licenses, they can tell the clerk that they wish to be organ and tissue donors. He or she will place a sticker on the back of the license. If someone changes his or her mind and decides they don't want to be an organ donor, they simply take the sticker off of their driver's license or destroy their donor card.

Signing a donor card indicates a desire to be a donor. However, when someone dies, the person's next-of-kin will still be asked to sign a consent form for donation. This is why it is important for people who wish to be organ donors to discuss this with their families and let their desires be known.

FRAUDULENT HEALTH ADVERTISING

Fake or fraudulent health products are not new. In early America, traveling "medicines shows" sold "snake oil" or "Indian Medicine" guaranteed to cure everything from cancer to baldness. We laugh at these claims today, but they are not much different than some infomercials on television, which advertise products that simply don't do what is promised. Some products are guaranteed to help you lose weight without exercise or restricting your calorie intake. Other commercials advertise equipment guaranteed to give you a muscular body without strenuous exercise.

Fake advertising is illegal, but commercials are worded carefully so they imply a product works without actually saying it. One trick is to hire a muscular man to demonstrate a muscle-building device. The viewer believes the man became muscular by using the device. In fact, the man probably never saw the device before he made the commercial. He probably became muscular by lifting weights for several years. Another trick is to hire a thin woman for a weight reduction commercial and show an old photograph that has been altered to make her look fat. The viewer is supposed to believe the model lost all of the weight by using the advertised product.

The next time you see a commercial for a questionable health product on television, watch carefully. While the narrator makes claims about the product as the model demonstrates it, watch the bottom of the screen. Most likely you will see a message in small print, which will flash on the screen almost too quickly to be read. The message will say, "Results may vary," or "These results are not typical." These messages are called **disclaimers.** What they really mean is, "This product probably won't work for you." Disclaimers are included in the commercial so the advertiser can say he warned the customers the product doesn't do what the commercial claims it will.

How can you spot a fraudulent commercial or advertisement for a medical or health-related product? It is not easy. We expect a commercial or advertisement to exaggerate a little, but if you see one that makes the following claims, beware:

The product is only available through mail order. If the product were offered by a large, reliable firm, it probably would be available at your local drug store or discount store.

It promises to do something you thought was impossible. Claims to restore hair to people who are bald, claims to let you eat whatever you want and still lose weight, and claims to build muscles or give you a flat stomach without strenuous exercise should all be looked upon as suspicious.

There are testimonials from people who have used the product. The people are likely to be hired actors or relatives of the manufacturer.

Words like "miracle" or "breakthrough" are used. If this product were really a miracle you wouldn't be seeing it on a commercial, you would be seeing it on the evening news.

It claims the product is "all natural." Many people believe that if it is all natural, it must be good. They also believe that if it is all natural, it certainly can't hurt them.

It uses fear to sell the product. They might say that if you don't use the product, you won't live as long, you'll feel bad, or you won't be attractive to the opposite sex.

Name _____ Date _____

WRITE A FRAUDULENT COMMERCIAL

You may have seen fraudulent commercials on television. Now, here's your chance to create one. Make up a fraudulent or fake health product, medicine, or machine, and then create a television commercial to sell it. You don't have to be too serious. You might want to make up a product that is so silly that no one would consider buying it. The purpose of this assignment is to gain a better understanding of commercials and the tactics advertisers use in order to get people to buy their products.

Answer the following questions before you write your commercial.

1. What is the name of the product? _____
2. What is the purpose of the product? _____
3. How is the product used? _____
_____
4. What is the cost of the product? _____
5. How was the product discovered or invented? _____
_____
6. How do the customers get the product? _____
_____
7. What advertising tactics will you use in your commercial? Here is a list of some of the tactics, sometimes called "appeals," that advertisers sometimes use.

   • This product will make you younger, more attractive, smarter, or stronger.
   • This product will make you healthy or allow you to live longer.
   • This product will make your life more interesting.
   • This product is being used by millions of people, some of them famous.
   • Smart, attractive, or mature people use this product.
   • This product is fun to use, or it gives you pleasure.
   • This product will solve all of your problems.
   • If you don't use this product, terrible things will happen.

   List the tactics or appeals you intend to use: _____
   _____
   _____
   _____

Use the form on the next page to create your commercial. The left side of the form is for the video, or what the audience will see during the commercial. The right side of the form is for the audio. The audio is the sound or narration the audience will hear during the commercial. You may need to make a copy of the form if you have more information to include. When you are finished, you may want to get a video camera and tape the commercial to be shown in class.

Name _____ Date _____

FRAUDULENT MEDICAL COMMERCIAL	
VIDEO	**AUDIO**

Safety and First Aid

Accidents are responsible for the greatest number of deaths among children and a high number of deaths among adults. Obviously, prevention is the best measure against accidents. As you look around your home and school, here are some hazards you might find that injure many people.

Falls occur frequently in a home. Open windows, unlatched doors leading to the basement or stairs, toys or other objects on the floor, slippery floors, and unanchored rugs or carpets are all major causes of falls in the home. Bathroom falls are also common. Rubber mats or abrasive treads in the bathtub or shower will eliminate many of these accidents.

Fires, burns, and electric shocks can cause injuries that will last a lifetime or even result in death. The most important rule in surviving a house fire is to be prepared. Have smoke detectors, check the batteries in them frequently, and be prepared to react at the first indication of a fire. Have an escape route in mind so that every family member knows what to do if there is a fire in the house.

Burns can be avoided by keeping flammable items out of reach of children. When using a cooking range, use the back burners and turn handles to the rear. You should also make sure the temperature on the water heater is adjusted so it will not scald someone turning on the hot water.

Unplugging appliances when they are not in use will help in avoiding electrical shocks, and keeping appliances that are plugged into an electrical source away from a water source will help avoid electrocution.

Accidental **poisoning** in the home is a hazard that occurs more frequently among children than adults. Carelessly stored household liquids such as bleach, detergents, dyes, insecticides, paints, and other items can cause poisoning. Poisonous items should be stored separately from food. They should be placed in a location that is inaccessible to children and should be kept in their original containers. Poisoning frequently occurs when a child swallows an adult's prescription medicine. Child-resistant lids for medicine are helpful, but it is also wise to store medicine out of sight and out of reach of children.

Firearms are very dangerous. They should not be touched or examined without adult supervision. While your parents may keep their firearms unloaded and safely stored in a locked cabinet, not all people do. Some people keep firearms loaded and easily accessible. If you are at a friend's house and they have a gun, it is best to leave immediately, even though they may assure you the gun is not loaded.

Many homes have **environmental hazards.** Environmental hazards are substances that can cause sickness or death when breathed or eaten. **Lead** is a pollutant that is sometimes found in the drinking water of some older homes. Homes built before 1970 may have lead in the paint. Lead poisoning can cause mental retardation and other health problems, especially in children. **Asbestos** was frequently used in building materials such as insulation. Asbestos fibers can cause respiratory disorders. **Radon** is a radioactive gas that can cause lung damage. **Carbon monoxide** poisoning occurs from unvented gasoline and kerosine stoves or automobile exhaust. It can cause death in a short amount of time. **Secondhand tobacco smoke** can cause respiratory illnesses and increase one's risk of developing cancer.

FIRST AID AND YOUR BODY

When an accident or emergency occurs, it is important for those present to be able to quickly help someone who is injured. Shown below are some common injuries and a very brief explanation of their treatments. After first aid treatment has been administered, a physician should treat the injury.

Ear Injuries
Stay lying down. Turn the head to the side with the injury to allow fluids to drain. Seek medical attention immediately.

Poisoning
Call your local Poison Control Center and follow their instructions carefully.

Drowning
Perform CPR if necessary. Remove wet clothing, and wrap in dry blankets.

Electrical Shock
Do not touch a person while he remains in contact with the current. Lay the person on his back, and loosen tight clothing. Elevate legs 8 to 12 inches and cover with a blanket.

Burns
Immerse in cold water. Blot dry with clean cloth, and cover with clean cloth. Elevate the burn higher than the heart.

Fractures and dislocations
Immobilize with padded splint, and remain as still as possible until medical aid arrives.

Bleeding, cuts, and wounds
Wash with soap and water. Apply direct pressure to control bleeding, and cover with sterile bandage.

Eye Injuries
Gently place a towel-covered ice bag over the eye. Consult a doctor immediately.

Choking
Perform Heimlich Maneuver, and seek medical attention.

Heart Attack
Place victim on his back, and loosen clothing. Open airway, and, if necessary, start CPR. Seek medical attention immediately.

Shock
Lay the person on his back, and loosen tight clothing. Elevate legs 8 to 12 inches, and cover with a blanket.

Bites and Stings
For a mild bite, wash with soap and water. If the skin is punctured or if there is pain, swelling, burning, or an allergic reaction, see a physician immediately.

Muscle Cramp
Stretch muscle and apply pressure. Apply warm, wet compresses and rest.

Sprains and Strains
Apply towel-wrapped ice bag for 15 to 30 minutes. Immobilize with a splint, and rest for 24 hours.

Name _____ Date _____

POISON

Listed below are several suggestions that will reduce the risk of accidental poisoning. In the space below each statement, write the reason for the suggestion.

1. Keep household products in their original containers. Never store antifreeze, paint, gasoline, or any other substance in soft-drink bottles, cups, or glasses.

_____

2. Store medicines, vitamins, and dietary supplements separate from household products.

_____

3. When disposing of old medicine, do not discard the old medicine in its container into the trash. Flush the old medication down the drain or toilet, and then rinse the container before discarding it.

_____

4. Don't take medication in the presence of children.

_____

5. Turn on the light when taking or dispensing medicine.

_____

6. Be sure all medicine is properly labeled.

_____

7. Never encourage children to take medicine by calling it "candy."

_____

8. Store food and household products in separate places.

_____

9. Store medicines and household products out of sight and out of reach of children or locked in a cabinet.

_____

10. Purchase household products that have child resistant packaging.

_____

HEALTH NOTEBOOK   Name _____ Date _____

FIRE ESCAPE PLAN

What would you do if there was a fire in your home? Do you have an escape plan? You should. In the space below, draw a floor plan of your home, and trace two escape routes for each room. Use arrows to indicate the directions your paths would take. Place large "Xs" where your smoke detectors are located.

First Floor

Second floor

78

Name _____ Date _____

HOME HAZARDS

Examine this diagram and discuss with the class or list on your own paper the safety hazards you see in this home. What should be done to make the house safer?

PREPARING FOR EMERGENCIES

The chances of you or a loved one surviving an emergency are greater if you are prepared. Here is an example. Suppose your sister runs into the house and says she has just been stung by a bee. She is crying, her arm is swelling, and she faints. What do you do? You call 911. When the paramedics arrive, they begin asking you questions about your sister's medical history. "Has she ever had this reaction to bee stings before? Is she taking any medicine? Does she have chronic diseases such as diabetes or asthma? Does she have any allergies?" Could you answer all of these questions for each family member in an emergency? Most of us couldn't. That is why it is best to keep a record of important health facts for each family member.

Fill out the following Medical Record Chart for yourself and any family members you would like and store them in your health notebook.

80

HEALTH NOTEBOOK

MEDICAL RECORD

Name _____ **Date of Birth** _____

    Address _____

    Phone at Home _____ **Phone at Work or School** _____

Primary Physician: _____

    Office Phone: _____ Home Phone: _____

Specialist: _____

    Office Phone: _____ Home Phone: _____

Dentist: _____

    Office Phone: _____ Home Phone: _____

Existing or Chronic Medical Problems: _____

_____

Allergies: _____

Blood Type: _____

Medicines:

    Name _____ For _____ Dosage _____

    Name _____ For _____ Dosage _____

    Name _____ For _____ Dosage _____

    Name _____ For _____ Dosage _____

Recent Hospitalizations, Injuries, or Medical Problems: _____

_____

Recent Immunizations: _____

_____

Emergency Numbers:

    Fire Department: _____ Ambulance: _____

    Poison Control Center: _____ Hospital Emergency Room: _____

    Relative or close friend: _____

        Office Phone: _____ Home Phone: _____

    Relative or close friend: _____

        Office Phone: _____ Home Phone: _____

Medical Insurance:

    Company Name: _____

        Phone: _____

    Address: _____

    Policy Number: _____

Name _____ Date _____

DEALING WITH EMERGENCIES

How well are you prepared to deal with emergencies? It is best to plan what you should do *before* an emergency occurs so that you can act immediately. Here are some questions that will help you decide what to do if you are faced with an emergency.

1. You are baby sitting with a toddler, and before the parents leave, they tell you that you should give the baby a bath before you put her to bed. What safety precautions should you take to protect the child?

_____

_____

2. You are riding your bicycle on a busy street. You have been taught that you should ride on the right side of the road, driving with the traffic. However, your friend who is riding with you says it is safer to ride on the left so you can see the oncoming traffic and pull off the road, if necessary. Who is right? Why?

_____

_____

3. You are hiking in the woods, and you see a baby animal all alone. He appears to be lost and you wonder if you should pick him up, take him home, and take care of him. What should you do?

_____

_____

4. When you arrive home from school, you see that your house is on fire. The fire doesn't seem to be too bad, and you feel that you can probably go inside and save some things. Is this a wise decision?

_____

_____

5. You are at the shopping mall when a terrible electrical storm occurs. You know your mother will worry so you decide to call her and let her know you are okay. Is this the wise thing to do?

_____

_____

6. You are riding home on your bike during an electrical storm. What should you do?

_____

_____

Name _____ Date _____

DEALING WITH EMERGENCIES (CONTINUED)

7. You see a tornado approaching. What should you do?

   At home: _____

   _____

   Outdoors: _____

   _____

   At work or school: _____

   _____

8. It is extremely hot and humid, but you decide to mow the lawn. When you are finished, you feel a little sick, so you decide to take a cold shower to cool off. Is this a good idea?

   _____

   _____

9. Your school has just received a bomb threat. As you are evacuating the building, you see a suspicious-looking package. What should you do?

   _____

   _____

10. You are caught in a flash flood. On your way home, you find that a dry creek you always cross has become flooded. The water does not appear to be deep, but it is moving rapidly. Is it safe to wade across?

   _____

   _____

11. Your family is driving down the highway, and you see an accident. A tanker truck has collided with a passenger car. The truck is overturned, and a liquid is spilled on the highway. What should you and your family do?

   _____

   _____

WRITE A RESEARCH PAPER

Write a research paper on some aspect of health, fitness, and staying well. You may choose your own topic or select one of the topics shown below. Your teacher may give you a list of health organizations and their toll-free telephone numbers that will provide you information on your topic. She may also give you a list of Internet addresses, which might be a starting point for your research.

1. Some countries have a national health plan, which means that citizens can visit doctors and be treated whenever they are sick. Most medical costs are paid by taxes. Should the United States have such a plan?

2. How healthy is a vegetarian diet?

3. Each year many people, especially children, die because they used a product that was poorly made. Should manufacturers be responsible for their products and pay the medical bills of those who are injured because of their products? Should manufacturers also need to pay victims an additional amount for "pain and suffering"?

4. Occasionally, the police set up a "road block" and stop cars in order to see if the car's lights, turn signals, horns, and other parts are working safely. The police call these road blocks "safety checks." What the police sometimes find is the driver has been drinking alcohol, and the police may arrest him. Some people are happy to have impaired drivers off the road, but others say the Constitution of the United States prohibits the police from stopping a car if it is not breaking any law. What do you think?

5. Fasting, or not eating for a certain period of time, is a controversial topic. Some say fasting is a healthy thing to do, while others disagree. What do you think?

6. Health care is one of a family's biggest expenses. Devise a plan that would help a family spend its heath care money wisely.

7. A person has atherosclerosis. What options are available to him or her? Which is best?

8. Some people feel that if a person who dies is frozen in liquid nitrogen immediately after death, scientists will be able to revive the patient in the future and then treat the illness that killed them. This branch of research is called cryogenics. Explain this research, and give your opinion.

9. What is alcoholism? What are its causes and treatments?

10. Explain the dangers of riding a bicycle. Outline a bicycle safety program.

11. Investigate several fast food restaurants. How healthy is the food? Are there healthy food choices at these restaurants?

12. Study a major disease such as polio, smallpox, or tuberculosis. Explain the disease, how the disease used to be treated, and how it is treated now.

13. Write about sleep. What is sleep? How important is it? How does one go about getting a good night's sleep?

Internet Health Sites

Achoo: Provides links to general health and medical sites.
http://www.achoo.com/

All About Health Magazine: Provides health information and features HealthLinx, which provides links to thousands of health sources on the Internet.
http://www.aliabouthealth.corn/

American Academy of Pediatrics: This site provides information about childhood illnesses, diseases, and research.
http://www.aap.org/

American Dental Association: Provides facts about the care of teeth.
http://www.ada.org/

American Medical Association: Provides information about various medical topics.
http://www.ama-assn.org/

Ash Web Page: Gives a timeline and explains important events related to smoking.
http://www.setinc.com/ash/

Ask the Dietitian: Provides information on nutrition.
http://www.dietitian.com

Centers for Disease Control and Prevention: Provides statistics and other information on various health issues.
http://www.cdc.gov/

Cyberspace Hospital: Provides links to sources of health care information throughout the world.
http://CH.nus.sg/CWch.html

Diseases and Disorders: Contains a search engine for finding information on various diseases.
http://www.mic.ki.se/Diseases/index.html

Duke University Healthy Devil On-Line: Applicable to anyone with questions about nutrition, sex, drinking, smoking, and other topics.
http://gilligan.mc.duke.edu/h-devil/

Fast Food Finder: Allows you to scan the menus of 15 restaurants for low-fat, low-calorie, low-sodium fast foods.
http://www.olen.com/food/

First Aid Online: Provides information for treatment of injuries and links to other health sources.
http://www.prairienet.org/~autumn/firstaid/

Food and Drug Administration: Provides food, drug, and general health information.
http://www.fda.gov/

Foot and Ankle Web Index: Provides information about foot and ankle problems.
http//www.footandankle.com/

Food and Nutrition Digest: http://www.oznet.ksu.edu/ext_f&n/newslet.htm

The Food Pyramid Guide: http://www.ganesa.com/food/index.html

Global Health Network: Provides links to health organizations and information resources around the world.
http://info.pitt.edu/HOMF_/GHNet/GHNet.html

Good Health Web: Lists health organizations in the United States.
http://www.social.com/health/

Hardin Meta Directory of Internet Health Sources: Provides an index of Internet links on various health topics.
http://www.arcade.uiowa.edu/hardin-www/md.html

Health A to Z: Contains a database on thousands of health topics.
http://www.healthatoz.com/

Internet Health Sites (continued)

Health on the Web: Helps consumers find health information.
http://www.healthfinder.gov

Healthwise: A health education and wellness program offered by Columbia University Health Service. Features a question-and-answer program.
http://www.columbia.edu/cu/healthwise/

Internet Mental Health: Provides overviews of mental disorders and treatments of the most common mental problems.
http://www.mentalhealth.com

Join Together: Provides information on the problems associated with tobacco, illegal drugs, and excessive use of alcohol.
http://www.jointogether.org

Joslin Diabetes Center: Provides information about diabetes.
http://www.joslin .harvard.edu/

Liszt: The Mailing List Directory: Contains a searchable database of more than 71,000 mailing lists, including various health topics.
http://www.Liszt.com/

Lycos Top 5 Percent: Lists the top 5 percent of what it believes are the "most useful" websites concerning family health.
http://point.lycos.com/reviews/database/hmfm_e.htm

Medical Mall: Provides information about pediatric health care.
http://www.rain.org/-medmall/

Medical Matrix: Provides links to various health sites.
http://www.slackinc.corn/matrix/

MedicineNet: Provides information and links on various health topics, including a medical dictionary.
http://www.medicinenet.com/

Medscape: Provides articles dealing with medical issues.
http://www.medscape.com/

Medsurf: Contains a searchable database of various health topics.
http://www. medsurf.com/

National Library of Medicine: Useful for finding health sources.
http://www.nlm.nih.gov/

OncoLink: One of the best web sites for cancer information.
http://www. oncolink.upenn.edu/

Online Health Network: The Mayo Clinic's information center.
http://healthnet.ivi.com/

USDA Nutrient Values: Provides the nutrient values of more than 5,000 foods.
http://www.rahul.net/cgibin/fatfree/usda/usda.cgi

Vitamin Update Consumer Information: Provides the most recent information about vitamins and minerals.
http://www.ozemail.com.au/~bookman/index.html

Wellness Web: Provides facts about conventional medicine, nutrition, and fitness.
http://www.wellweb.com/

World Health Organization: Provides world health topics, statistics, and advice.
http://www.who.ch/

Answer Keys

Heredity and Eye Color (page 9)

1.

2. Answers will vary but should include something like: The odds are that only brown-eyed babies will be produced in the second generation. According to Mendel's law, however, the third generation would be offspring of two brown-eyed parents who carry a recessive gene for blue eyes. The third generation will likely have three times as many brown-eyed children as blue-eyed children.

Exercises For Different Age Groups (page 17)

Stress the need for a physical examination before beginning any exercise program. The answers given below are only representative of the kinds of exercises that might be appropriate. Your students will think of other appropriate exercises.

1. Weight lifting is the best, but other exercises might include canoeing, boxing, skiing, swimming, tennis, skating, rowing and running.
2. Aerobic exercises, biking, rowing, running, walking, jogging, tennis, skating, swimming, and skipping rope.
3. Walking, dancing, bowling, gardening, and golf might be the exercises he begins with, and as his health improves, his physician will probably recommend more strenuous exercises.
4. Walking, dancing, bowling, aerobic exercises, skiing, golf, jogging, running, tennis, and swimming.
5. Gardening, walking, dancing, appropriate aerobic exercise, swimming, and yoga.
6. Aerobic exercise, dancing, gardening, golf, tennis, swimming, rowing, yoga, and appropriate weight lifting.

Exercise Quiz (page 21)

1. F	14. F
2. F	15. F
3. T	16. T
4. F	17. T
5. T	18. F
6. T	19. T
7. F	20. T
8. T	21. T
9. F	22. F
10. T	23. T
11. F	24. T
12. F	25. T
13. F	

Communicable Diseases Quiz (pages 23–24)

1. Influenza
2. Colds
3. Chicken Pox
4. Acquired Immune Deficiency Syndrome (AIDS)
5. Measles
6. Mononucleosis
7. Hepatitis
8. Lice
9. Scabies
10. Mumps
11. Ringworm
12. Pneumonia
13. Strep Throat
14. Tonsillitis
15. Tuberculosis
16. Sty

Factors That Cause Cancer (page 27)

1. Smoking
2. Ultraviolet Rays
3. Alcohol
4. Chewing Tobacco
5. Radiation
6. Diet
7. Estrogen
8. Environmental Hazard

Noncommunicable Diseases and Disorders Quiz (page 28)

1. Bronchitis
2. Cerebral Palsy
3. Scoliosis
4. Anorexia Nervosa
5. Appendicitis
6. Muscular Dystrophy
7. Asthma
8. Sickle-Cell Anemia
9. Diabetes
10. Rheumatoid Arthritis
11. Down Syndrome
12. Tendinitis
13. Epilepsy
14. Hemophilia
15. Pleurisy

Smoking Crossword Puzzle (page 31)

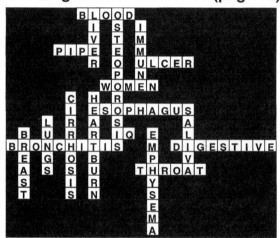

Substance Abuse Discussion Questions (pages 39–41)

These questions are designed to be discussed in class. The answers will vary, but as a class, some of the better answers can be identified and examined.

Nutrition True-False Test (page 46)

1. trace
2. True
3. celluloid
4. vegetables
5. True

6. True
7. nutritionist
8. Proteins
9. True
10. True
11. True
12. minerals
13. starches
14. fat soluble
15. True

Identify the Food Groups (page 48)
1. C   2. F   3. D   4. B
5. D   6. B   7. C   8. A
9. E   10. A   11. E   12 C
13. A   14. B   15. D   16. B
17. C   18. D   19. F   20. E
21. A   22. F   23. E   24. D

The ABCs of Nutrition (pages 49–50)
A. anorexia
B. bulimia
C. carbohydrate
D. dairy
E. egg yolk
F. fiber
G. grain
H. heart disease
I. iron
J. junk foods
K. kidneys
L. LDL cholesterol
M. metabolism
N. niacin
O. osteoporosis
P. protein
Q. quota
R. RDA
S. saturated
T. tooth decay
U. unsaturated fat
V. vegetarian
W. water
X. xylem
Y. yogurt
Z. zinc

Interpreting Food Labels (pages 57–58)
1. Caramel Popcorn
2. Chicken Noodle Soup
3. Cake Mix
4. Sugar
5. Chicken Stock
6. Sugar
7. Brown Sugar
8. Enriched Egg Noodles
9. Enriched flour bleached
10. B
11. A
12. C
13. C
14. B
15. C
16. A
17. C
18. C
19. C
20. C
21. C
22. C
23. A
24. A
25. A
26. So the consumer is able to make an informed choice concerning food.
27. B. Soup would be a better choice than caramel popcorn or cake. It provides more of the good ingredients and less of the bad ingredients.

Weight Reduction (page 60)
1. Five reasons U.S. citizens are more obese:
Possible answers include:
a. People in other countries get more exercise. They have fewer labor-saving devices. They walk to work or to the market. Even in affluent countries, the cost of gasoline causes many people to use bicycles rather than drive.
b. People in other countries eat less meat and cheese and more grain. In the United

89

States, meat is served at most meals. People in other countries build their meals around bread, rice, or potatoes.

c. People in other countries, for the most part, eat only at meal time. In the United States, people are constantly snacking.

d. People in the United States eat larger portions than those in other countries. This is especially true of high calorie items such as meat.

e. People in other countries eat meals that contain less fat. Since food that has a high fat content often costs more, it is eaten less in less affluent countries.

f. People in other countries don't often include dessert at the end of their meals. When dessert that contains a high amount of calories is served, it is usually for special occasions. Generally, however, a dessert in other countries is often a piece of fruit.

2. List four causes of obesity.
Possible answers include:

a. Lack of exercise.

b. Unhealthy eating habits: eating too much or eating high-calorie foods.

c. Genetic: If the parents are obese, it is more likely the children will be obese. Also, some families tend to eat more or prefer high-calorie foods.

d. Psychological and physical changes: Eating is sometimes used to relieve stress. Obesity may also be related to certain drugs or medicines, or it might be the result of a glandular problem.

3. List five diseases or health problems associated with obesity or being overweight.
Possible answers include:

a. Heart disease

b. Diabetes

c. High blood pressure

d. Some cancers

e. Diseases of bones and joints

f. Gout

g. Skin diseases

h. Sleepiness and fatigue

i. Psychological effects

4. List ten healthy ways to lose weight permanently.
Possible answers include:

a. Increase your level of activity. Walk instead of driving.

b. Eat less meat, cheese, and sweets.

c. Eat more grains, fruits, and vegetables.

d. Cut out snacking.

e. Eat smaller portions.

f. Eat more slowly. You'll enjoy the meal more, and you can stop when you are full.

g. Stop eating when you are no longer hungry.

h. Don't eat desserts, or substitute with fruit or a low-calorie dessert.

i. Don't buy or keep treats or snacks at home.

j. Don't drink alcoholic beverages. Alcohol adds a lot of calories, but no nutrients.

k. Begin a meal with low-calorie hot soup. You will eat more slowly, and it fills you up.

l. Choose low-calorie and low-fat sauces, dressings, and other foods.

m. Don't eat everything on your plate.

n. Use non-stick pans when cooking. This reduces the need for cooking with fat.

o. Drink eight glasses of water a day. A beverage before and during your meal will help you feel full faster and longer.

p. Limit your intake of fried foods.

q. Don't feel you need to eat everything left on the table so it isn't thrown away.

r. Limit your intake of fast foods and processed foods.

Handling Stress and Depression (page 64)
1. You should talk to your friend and listen to him. If he says something that might lead you to believe that he might be considering

suicide, you should talk to an adult in order to get Ahmad help.

2. This isn't true. Most people who attempt suicide tell someone else of their intentions. You should take them seriously and refer them to someone equipped to handle the problem most effectively.

3. Yes, these are all signs that could indicate a person is considering suicide. The sudden change from extreme depression to being at peace may mean she has made the decision to kill herself. It is another sign to be concerned about.

4. Tell him, "I don't want you to die. You are my friend." Ask him to promise he won't try to commit suicide again. Tell him if he is ever unhappy and considers hurting himself, he should talk to you or someone else first.

5. Call his parents immediately.

6. You should not try to "rescue" her or try to handle the situation on your own. You can help her best by talking to an adult who will refer her to someone who has been trained to deal with these problems.

7. Yes, if he is serious about hurting himself, he may not tell you the truth. Get Bill help. If you don't know where to turn, chances are there are a number of 24-hour anonymous telephone counseling or suicide prevention hotlines.

Health Care Workers (page 67)

1. Immunologist
2. Cardiologist
3. Psychologist
4. Optometrist
5. Anesthesiologist
6. Podiatrist
7. Obstetrician
8. Dermatologist
9. Internist
10. Gynecologist
11. Dentist
12. Plastic surgeon
13. Geriatrician
14. Chiropractor
15. Pathologist
16. Allergist
17. Pediatrician
18. Primary care physician
19. Radiologist
20. Neurologist
21. Surgeon
22. Orthopedist
23. Orthodontist

Poison (page 77)

Answers are evident, but they may vary somewhat.

Dealing With Emergencies (pages 82–83)

1. Test the bath water before putting the child into the tub. Make sure there are no small appliances plugged in near the tub. Make sure you hold the child when he or she is standing in the tub. Don't leave the child unattended in the tub.

2. You are. You should ride with the traffic, not against it. A large percentage of bicycle/car accidents occur because someone is riding against the traffic. Automobile drivers expect all vehicles, including bikes, to be moving in the same direction and in the correct lane. When they are not in the correct lane, drivers sometimes do not know what the biker intends to do.

3. Avoid the animal. It might be diseased, and even if it isn't, if you pick it up, the animal might bite or scratch you. Also, it is unlikely the animal is lost. Its mother is probably close by. She might attack you if you get too close to her baby. Finally, it is not wise to try to care for a wild animal. They can cause injury to your family or friends, and they probably would not survive in captivity.

4. No. The fire may be much worse than it appears. Also, most victims of fires do not die of the flames, but of poisonous gases they breathe when they are in a burning

house. The smoke-filled home would probably make it impossible for you to find what you were looking for anyway. Nothing in the house is more valuable than your life.

5. Do not use the telephone or any electrical appliances during a storm. You can be shocked or killed. Telephone lines, wires, and metal pipes can conduct electricity.

6. Get off your bike and find a building as quickly as possible. Your bike could act as a lightning rod. If there is no building, squat low to the ground as quickly as possible. Never seek shelter beneath a single large tree in the open. Stay away from bodies of water. If you are in a level field and feel your hair stand on end, bend forward, crouch, and put your hands on your knees. Do not lie flat on the ground. When your hair stands on end, it means that lightning is about to strike.

7a. Go to the basement, storm cellar, or the lowest level of the building. If there is no basement, you should go to an inner hallway or a smaller room without windows, such as a bathroom or closet. Stay away from the windows. Get under a piece of heavy furni-

ture. If you are in a mobile home and you have time, find shelter somewhere else.

b. If possible, find shelter inside a building. If you can't find a building, lie in a ditch. Cover your head and neck.

c. Go to the basement or to an inside hallway at the lowest level. Stay away from large open areas such as auditoriums, cafeterias, and large hallways. If possible, get under a piece of sturdy furniture

8. Avoid strenuous activity during extremely hot temperatures. A cold shower when you are hot and overheated can cause hypothermia.

9. You should not touch any suspicious package. Evacuate the area around the package, and notify the authorities immediately.

10. Never walk through flood waters. Even water a few inches deep can sweep you off your feet if it is moving fast enough.

11. Stay away from the accident and help keep others away. Do not walk in or touch any of the spilled liquid. Try not to inhale gases, fumes, or smoke.